APPLYING TO COLLEGE FOR STUDENTS WITH ADD OR LD

A Guide to Keep You
(and Your Parents)
Sane, Satisfied, and Organized
Through the Admission Process

378.161
GRO

To all my students and teachers, past, present, and future, and to my family. This book would not have been possible without the dedication and talent of my editors, Becky Shaw and Kristine Enderle. Thanks for believing in the project and working so hard to make it a reality. —BG

Published by
MAGINATION PRESS
An Educational Publishing Foundation Book
American Psychological Association
750 First Street, NE
Washington, DC 20002

For more information about our books, including a complete catalog, please write to us, call 1-800-374-2721, or visit our website at www.apa.org/pubs/magination.

Book and cover design by
Silverander Communications, Santa Barbara, CA
Printed by Sheridan Books, Ann Arbor, MI.

Library of Congress Cataloging-in-Publication Data
Grossberg, Blythe N.
Applying to college for students with ADD or LD : a guide to keep you (and your parents) sane, satisfied, and organized through the admission process / by Blythe Grossberg.
p. cm.

ISBN-13: 978-1-4338-0892-0 (pbk. : alk. paper)
ISBN-10: 1-4338-0892-7 (pbk. : alk. paper) 1. Universities and colleges—United States—Admission. 2. College applications—United States. 3. Learning disabled teenagers—Education (Higher)
I. American Psychological Association. II. Title.
LB2351.2 .G77

378.1′61087--dc22

2010023130

10 9 8 7 6 5 4 3 2 1

APPLYING TO COLLEGE FOR STUDENTS WITH ADD OR LD

A Guide to Keep You (and Your Parents) Sane, Satisfied, and Organized Through the Admission Process

BY **BLYTHE GROSSBERG, PSYD**

MAGINATION PRESS ◉ WASHINGTON, DC

AMERICAN PSYCHOLOGICAL ASSOCIATION

CONTENTS

HOW TO USE THIS BOOK

Welcome to the college application process. You've probably already heard a lot about it. You may have seen older students or siblings go through the process, and people at your school may have talked about where students got into college at the end of their senior year. What a lot of people concentrate on is the end result—admission to a specific college. However, there is a lot that has to happen before the admission. In fact, it's best to think of the college application process as a long journey that takes you where you want to go. Each person's journey is different, and each person has different challenges and opportunities along the way.

This book is written expressly to help you, students with ADD or learning disabilities (LD), succeed in the college environment. More students with identified learning disabilities than ever before are attending—and succeeding at—colleges across the nation. In fact, five times the number of students with learning disabilities now enter college than they did in the 1980s. Every school—from small liberal arts colleges to the Ivy League to large state universities to community colleges—has students with ADD and LD. College professors and administrators have become more enlightened over the past several years about learning issues and ADD, and they willingly accept students with these types of profiles.

7

Learning differences might be a better way to describe what are generally called disabilities. (But for the purpose of this book, we'll still refer to them as learning disabilities or LD.) Yes, people who have ADD or ADHD may struggle with inattention and impulsivity and may not be so thrilled with school at times. But they are also generally creative, out-of-the-box thinkers who bring a fresh perspective to all that they do. People with dyslexia are often gifted in a variety of fields, such as art, design, and math. In addition, students who have other types of learning differences have generally had to work diligently in high school. (Does this sound familiar?) As a result, they have the skills and motivation to do well in college, particularly when they can concentrate on academic areas that interest them. In other words, you have a lot going for you as you embark on the college application process. This book will point out how your learning differences may present opportunities and challenges throughout the application process, and it will help you consider how to use your strengths to your advantage.

Why This Book?

This book will help you organize your college application and decision-making process and assist you (and your parents) in finding a school that's right for you. This guide doesn't tell you what to do with a one-size-fits-all approach but instead allows you to figure out what's important to you in a college and helps to remind you of your priorities at each step of the admission process. It's chock full of charts, checklists, and assessments to keep you organized and on track. Here's a basic overview of the application process.

- The first step is for you to take a good look at yourself and what you offer to colleges.

- You will then think about how to build on your considerable strengths, how to correct some of your weaknesses, and how to confront some of your challenges.

- You will begin to build a portfolio of courses, grades, and extracurricular activities to present to colleges.

- You will discover, through an organized, thoughtful process, what matters to you most in choosing a college, and you will figure out which kinds of support you will need to thrive in college.

- Armed with this important information about yourself, in the spring of your junior year, you will start looking at and choosing potential colleges that could be right for you.

- Finally, you will get recommendations, fill out applications, tour schools, and interview. By the end of your senior year, you will choose the right college for you based on all the thought you've put into what makes you successful and committed.

If this process sounds daunting—don't worry. This book is a companion that will guide you step-by-step through the process and ask you questions that help you and your family choose a college that's right for you.

Using the Timeline & Checklist

Use this book over time to help you and your family structure the college application process. The timeline at the end of this section provides an overview of the entire process, so you can organize the steps you have to take well in advance. The checklist, on the other hand, is like your to-do list. Use the checklist to mark off each broad step as you complete it.

Applying to colleges and choosing which to attend is a lengthy and sometimes confusing journey. Turn to this book over your junior and senior years for guidance. Ideally, you should start looking over the timeline during the **end of your sophomore or beginning of your junior year.** (Don't worry if you can't get to everything by your sophomore year—you still have plenty of time.)

JUNIOR YEAR: PREPARATION & APPLICATION

The **summer before and fall of your junior year** is when you really start getting into the application process. That's when you start building your portfolio. In other words, it's when you will think about what you need to do to prepare for the college admission process, including building on your strengths and working on your challenges. You will also determine the most important priorities you are looking for in a college—before you start applying to schools. In addition, this book will help you organize your transcript, get set up with extracurriculars, and plan studying for and taking your standardized tests.

In the **final part (spring) of your junior year,** you'll identify specific qualities you want in a college and research which schools are right for you. You'll go on college tours and conduct in-depth (and interesting) investigations of colleges on these visits. You will think about some important questions to ask while touring schools—not only about academics but also about dorm life, food, and support systems—so you can really understand what it might be like to attend a specific school.

SENIOR YEAR: DECISION TIME

Work on the third section of this book during the **first part of your senior year** (but you should skim over it during your junior year to help you look ahead). This section will help you fill out your college applications, ask teachers for recommendations, and complete other parts of the college admission process.

As you go through this book (and application process), try to be

- honest with yourself, without being boastful,
- specific,
- realistic, and
- positive.

And good luck!

COLLEGE APPLICATION TIMELINE
SOPHOMORE YEAR
if you haven't done anything here, don't worry!

- Take the PSAT
- Think about classes for junior year
- Start thinking about college, talking to friends, and possibly touring schools
- Get involved with extracurricular activities that interest you
- Request accommodations on SATs and/or ACTs and other tests

JUNIOR YEAR

Fall	• Take the PSAT and study for the SAT or ACT • Request accommodations on SATs and/or ACTs and other tests if you haven't already • Sign up for SAT Subject Tests, if required • Sign up for classes in your strongest subject(s) • Athletes, start the recruiting process • Get involved with serious extracurriculars
Winter	• Take the SAT or ACT and Subject Tests, if required
Spring	• Start researching colleges • Tour schools and research their services • Go on virtual tours if you can't visit schools • College coaches may contact high school athletes about recruiting • Narrow down list of schools to a solid mix of about 10 • Sign up for senior classes
Summer	• Study for SAT or ACT, if retaking • Think of teachers and others who might write recommendations

Summer (continued)	• Start thinking about essay topics • Make sure your evaluation and documentation are up-to-date to request accommodations • Consider taking a gap year

SENIOR YEAR

August	• Arrange additional school visits • Start filling out the Common Application • Musicians and artists, compile portfolios • Decide if you want to apply early to college • Talk to your parents about finances
September–December	• Sign up for and (re)take the SAT, Subject Tests, or ACT • Fill out and submit applications in advance of deadlines (either regular and/or early admission) • Request recommendations • Fill out and submit financial aid forms • Apply for scholarships • Show college counselor list of schools • Prepare for and have interviews
January–March	• Relax and wait for responses from schools • Possibly continue to have interviews
April–May/June	• Receive responses from schools • Visit schools • Review financial aid packages and possibly ask schools to reconsider packages • Decide on school • Consider whether to remain on any wait lists

*Note that college coaches cannot contact high school athletes until the end of junior year, but speak with your high school coach about how to get on coaches' recruiting lists before that time.

APPLICATION CHECKLIST

Junior Year: Fall–Winter
Organizing Your Stats & Building Your Portfolio

- ☐ Do Your SWOT Analysis
- ☐ Optimize Your Transcript & GPA
- ☐ Get Involved in Extracurriculars
- ☐ Take Standardized Tests

Junior Year: Spring–Summer
Finding the Right College for You

- ☐ Prepare to Research Schools
- ☐ Develop a List of Schools
- ☐ Tour Colleges

Senior Year: Fall–Winter
Putting Together Your Application

- ☐ Organize Your Application Deadlines
- ☐ Get Recommendations
- ☐ Face Your Essay
- ☐ Complete Application Supplements
- ☐ Submit Applications
- ☐ Tackle Money Matters
- ☐ Go on Interviews

Senior Year: Spring

- ☐ Make Your Decision

JUNIOR YEAR: FALL–WINTER

ORGANIZING YOUR STATS & BUILDING YOUR PORTFOLIO

Applying to college is like the dating game. Colleges are looking for students who are good matches with their institutions. You will fare better in this dating game if you know

- what you have to offer,
- what you need to succeed, and
- how you'd like to develop in your college years.

In other words, who you are and what you want to be.

But before you even think about colleges, you need to think about yourself. Yes, you already know yourself, but you may not have considered your strengths and weaknesses thoroughly and objectively. These tools will help you to do just that. With this information, you'll build a portfolio—your collection of work and information that shows your talents, who you are, and how you've progressed. But what exactly is in this portfolio?

- Your strengths and weaknesses
- Your high school transcript
- Your extracurricular activities

- SAT or ACT scores (you'll generally take these in the winter or spring of your junior year—it's good to start prepping for them now)

- Recommendations from teachers and other adults in your community

So, in the fall of your junior year, you should be thinking of about the following (in the context of applying to college, of course!):

- What you are doing well and what you offer to colleges (your strengths)

- What you need to work on (your weaknesses)

- What you need to move forward (your opportunities)

- What might trip you up in college (your threats)

- What you'll need to be successful at college (your skills)

- What you want out of college (your goals)

CHAPTER 1

SWOT ANALYSIS

In order to determine which type of college would suit you best, you need to take stock of what you have achieved up until this point in high school and what your goals are before you head to college. A SWOT analysis is a look at your strengths, weaknesses, opportunities, and threats. You can figure out your strengths and weaknesses on your own or with the help of a supportive yet objective friend, relative, or teacher. Opportunities are the things that can help you—accommodations and areas in which you can advocate for yourself. Threats are, well, bad habits you might have picked up, things that can bite you if you're not careful about taking care of them. Having all this information about yourself is important—you will know where you stand right now and where you want to go.

From this SWOT analysis, you'll generate a plan about how to build on your already existing strengths. You'll also find ways around the inevitable weaknesses that each college applicant has.

Your Strengths

Many students with ADD or LD tend to feel negative about their school performance, even if there are areas in which they have excelled. Remember that in college, unlike in high school, you will be able to concentrate your studies more fully on what you like—and are most likely good at. At this point, you have to assess what you have achieved and establish realistic goals for the rest of high school and college.

You may find that you need a trusted friend or teacher to help you think about your strengths if you are very negative about your own performance. Don't forget to consider areas outside of academics, such as art, theater, music, sports, and jobs you've held. Keep in mind that many students with ADD or LD tend to have a better transcript as they move through school. That is, they may not have reached their full potential by their freshman year of high school. If you show this type of development, build on what has helped you to better your past performance. You'll want to analyze what helped you improve in the past so that you can use these same types of tools and supports in college.

As you jump into this process, grab a notebook or create a spreadsheet or Word doc to write down and save your ideas. And remember:

- **Try to think realistically** about how far you've gotten at this point in time. Present your achievements as they now stand, without embellishment or wishful thinking.

- **Be specific.** Use actual evidence—projects, papers, classes, camps, internships, awards, leadership experiences—to back up what you say. Don't just state that you have "leadership ability." Instead, write about how you organized a fundraising activity for a club, led a group of younger kids, or served as captain of your travel soccer team.

1. **What are my academic strengths?**

    Consider specific classes you've taken, particularly at the advanced level. Also consider specific papers you've written, projects you have undertaken, and academic work you have done outside of school.

2. **What are my extracurricular strengths?**

   Consider activities on which you've spent a great deal of time, such as clubs, service organizations, religious organizations, arts, and sports. For each activity, note whether you served in a leadership role.

3. **How can I build on my top strengths?**

   Try to come up with specific goals for your junior and senior years of high school that are realistic and that will allow you to build on your strengths. (You may need to consult a coach, teacher, parent, or friend in this process.)

Your Weaknesses

Consider the challenges that you must address as you prepare to apply to college. What areas do you need to work on? Though it is difficult sometimes to address your weaknesses, keep in mind that everyone has challenges and that you are still learning and growing. College is about continuing to develop, and no one expects you to have accomplished everything by the time you're 18. Instead, look at this as an exercise in planning for the future. Envisioning the next year or so in high school and the years in college, write down your challenges. Think about some ways to overcome what's holding you back.

As with your strengths, remember:

- **Be specific.** Don't simply say something like, "I'm stupid in Spanish." Instead, write something like, "I need to work on my Spanish grammar." Write "I need to create a planner system" rather than "I'm a totally disorganized mess."

- Try to be **constructive** about what you need to do to improve your skills before college. You again may need to work with a trusted teacher, parent, friend, counselor, or tutor to help you be objective.

1. **What academic areas do I need to improve?**

   Think about your difficult subjects, from history to math to English to chemistry. Be sure to list all of these even if you don't plan on studying a specific subject in college.

2. **How can I build the academic skills I'm lacking?**

   Think about specific strategies for each academic area of weakness. If English lit is a tough subject, think about ways you can build your critical reading and writing skills. You may need to ask your teachers to help you here. For example, is there a method your teacher recommends for improving your reading speed or retention or for revising your writing? Remember, these strategies will vary depending on your unique learning style and your specific LD(s).

3. **What are my organizational weaknesses?**

   Think about your time-management, study, and planning skills. Do you procrastinate? Do you have a hard time keeping track of assignments and your stuff? If so, now is the time to figure out how to become better organized before you head to college on your own.

4. **Do I have any social weaknesses I need to work on?**

   This is probably where you need an objective person who knows you well to help you. Are you

SHOULD YOU TAKE A GAP YEAR?

Are you burnt out with school? Face it—having ADD or LD makes school pretty tough. Consider if taking some time off would be good for you. Did you know taking time off before college can actually help you do much better in school? Many colleges even encourage students to take a gap year. Some schools have found that students who take a year off before matriculating arrive at campus more motivated and mature. And one school wants about 10% of its students to travel abroad to do service and learn about a foreign culture before they enter as first-year students. Colleges consider these experiences vital for future workers in an increasingly global world.

If you find yourself with a serious case of senioritis that simply doesn't go away before freshman year of college, consider the gap-year alternative. You can spend a year, or part of a year, studying abroad, traveling, performing community service, working, or doing an internship. These experiences can help you become more mature, boost your self-confidence, and improve your organizational and work skills. A gap year can also help you identify what you want to study in college.

really shy? Do you have a hard time talking to people or making friends? Do you sometimes have a hard time picking up on social cues? If so, there are ways to work on these issues if you recognize that they may be getting in your way.

Your Opportunities

One of the most important skills for college students with ADD or LD is the ability to advocate for themselves. Self-advocacy is about speaking up and asking for the accommodations you need to be successful in school. What will make you successful in college is the ability and confidence to ask for what you need in order to succeed. Find and make opportunities for yourself. This skill is perhaps the most difficult to develop. It's much more straightforward to develop your math or writing skills. Developing self-advocacy skills means that you have to admit that at times, you need accommodations or support to be successful. If you are ashamed of asking for help or if you believe that you can't be successful no matter what you do, then you probably won't feel entirely comfortable asking for what you need (or you won't ask at all).

Remember, your parents won't be with you in college to make sure that you ask your professor for extended time or that you check in with your dean to see which classes you should take. It's vital that you begin to develop the ability to do these things now, on your own, so that you are prepared for college and for your adult life.

Advocating for yourself—that is, asking for what you need—is a critical skill. When done in a respectful, open manner, self-advocacy enables you to get the help you need to be successful. In this exercise, consider how well you advocate for yourself to get what you need in high school.

1.   **Do you ask teachers for extra help outside of class?**

     If you are lost in class, how do you react? Do you just resign yourself to your confused fate, or do you try to get help? Do you let your teachers know if you have tried to understand the work on your own but still can't figure it out? Some students are really wary of seeming confused, but working with your teachers—asking good questions in class and meeting with teachers outside of class, if needed— is the way that students succeed.

2. **How exactly do you ask for help?**

   Do you ask for help in a way that shows your teachers that you are working hard and that you appreciate their time? Respectfully? Without being defensive or overly aggressive? Do you approach teachers with specific questions or with vague complaints, such as "I just don't get it!"? Don't alienate your teachers by blaming them for your poor grades or by making too many demands on their time. Remember, how you ask for help determines the quality of help you'll get.

3. **Do you work with a tutor or learning specialist on specific subjects or on study skills?**

   Do you go outside of school for help? Or do you feel that you always want to do everything yourself, even if it means struggling? Do you recognize that every student must ask for the right kinds of help at times? If you work with tutors, do you make sure that you do all the work on your own and let them teach you approaches to your work that will help you be more independent in the future?

4. **Which accommodations do you ask for at school?**

Are you receiving the types of accommodations, such as extra time on tests, that you need? Do you need other types of assistance but don't feel comfortable asking for them?

5. **What is your role in asking for these accommodations?**

Do you ask your parents to talk to your teachers to make sure that you receive the accommodations that you need? Or do you approach teachers yourself to arrange for these accommodations?

6. **How can you be more assertive to ask for what you need?**

ARE YOU UP TO SPEED ON YOUR IEP?

If you feel that you need to develop your ability to ask for help, consider meeting with your teachers and parents at your annual IEP (individualized educational plan) meeting (if you have such a meeting). IEP meetings are held with school administrators and teachers to determine the plan that will help you do well in school. Attend these meetings and become part of the process of understanding what you need—and asking for it. In addition, ask your parents if you can read your educational evaluation to understand what it says about you and how you learn. If you're part of these meetings, you will understand what helps you to succeed and how to ask for this type of help.

HEADS UP ❗ As part of the IDEA (Individuals with Disabilities Education Act) of 2004, IEPs must include transition services by the time a student is 16. That is, your IEP must

GET ORGANIZED!

A critical part of being successful in high school and college is organization and time management. The more structure and organization you have, the more control you'll have over your schedule and the more in control you'll feel. So what can you do?

- **Get a planner.** If you haven't been using a planner, now is the time to get one and customize it to your needs. Use a paper planner, a calendar on your smart phone or laptop, or all of these systems. The important thing is to choose a system that you will use.

- **Anticipate all your weekly activities.** These activities may include classes, work schedules, tutoring or medical appointments, extracurriculars, your social life, laundry time, etc.

- **Plan for tests at least a week in advance** by working a solid block of studying into your scheduled time. Cramming the night before a test is not the most effective way to learn the material (and it's really stressful).

- **Schedule specific times during the week when you will study.** Block off at least two hours during week nights and more on Sundays.

- **Figure out how to schedule time for studying and work** into your social and extracurricular calendar. Block off times for schoolwork and for other activities in your organizational system.

- **Break down each major assignment and plan ahead** for long-term work, such as research projects. You can put each short-term step into your planner, such as choosing a research topic, going to the library to get sources, writing a rough draft, and revising your work. Don't expect to complete your lengthy assignments the night before they are due.

contain specific plans about helping you make the transition to life after college. For more information, you can visit http://idea.ed.gov or consult your local school board. Be sure to work with your parents and members of your IEP team to develop a plan for moving from high school to college.

Your Threats

Your threats are your own worst enemies—unlike your weaknesses, they pose *potential*, not outright, problems. Your threats include the relatively weak skills that you need to work on over time. You might get by, but these threats can trip you up eventually. They include: less-than-ideal time management skills, poor organization, and other habits that might not let you achieve your best. A lot of students headed to college have less-than-ideal time-management skills, but when students are on their own in college, they need to be able to organize their academic work and fit it into a busy schedule that also involves socializing, sports, extracurricular activities, sleeping, doing laundry, and possibly working. Your junior year of high school is the time to start thinking about taking on these threats so that they don't get in your way when you head to college.

1. **Do you have poor time-management skills?**

    If you have poor time-management skills, start working on planning your activities now. Get a planner that you will use. You can use a paper planner, a smart phone, or a calendar on your computer. Be sure to schedule your work on a nightly basis and fit in all the other activities you need to do, including extracurriculars.

TELLING COLLEGES ABOUT YOUR ADD OR LD (OR NOT?)

The question about whether or not you should disclose your ADD or LD to college admissions offices is a tricky and personal one. If you've shown great improvement over your high school career—say, after you started taking medication for ADD or after you learned better study habits—you might want to consider declaring your ADD or LD. Here's why:

- **If you don't tell colleges about what you've had to overcome in the past**, they may simply assume your less-than-stellar record in the earlier days of your high school career is a product of your laziness or lack of talent.

- **College admissions offices want to see evidence of personal and academic growth** through your high school career. Learning strategies to deal with ADD or LD are prime examples of this type of growth. If you can show colleges that you've developed good study skills and matured in the process of working with and through your strengths and weakness, you will have a compelling story to tell them.

- **Colleges won't necessarily know that you've had accommodations in high school** such as extended time, and they do not know about accommodations on standardized tests. However, if you've had accommodations, such as a foreign language waiver in high school, colleges will automatically know this information when they look at your transcript and see that those courses are missing. Therefore, it may be more necessary to write a letter explaining your situation if you've had obvious accommodations.

2. Are you down about yourself?

Do you tend to get overly critical of yourself? If so, you may not even feel that you should ask for the help you need to be successful. In other words, if you feel that you simply can't do well in a certain subject, you may zone out in class or not even ask the teacher for extra help. You might even give up. Well, now is the time to get help—before you go through the sometimes difficult college application process. Seek out a trusted counselor, talk to your teachers, or go to your parents to help you assess what you need to work on—and to recognize your talents, not just your weaknesses.

3. Do you rely too much on your parents' help?

You may not want to credit your parents with much at this point in your high school career, but it's time to be honest about everything they do for you. All of these supports are going to be missing if you attend college away from home. Consider all the chores you are going to take on as a first-year college student. Try to take on some of these responsibilities yourself as your junior and senior years go on.

Analyze Your SWOT

Now is the time to sit down and look at your SWOT analysis. In this step, you'll use the information above to develop a list of the kinds of support you need in college—the support that works with your strengths and weaknesses, your opportunities and threats. (This exercise will help you determine what you need to look for in a college as you start conducting your research.)

Many students think that when they head to college, they will magically be able to handle all their work on their own and that turning 18 makes all of their challenges immediately go away. While high school and college help students develop better skills and move toward independence, most students—including those without LD and ADD—still need support, particularly in their first year of college.

SUPPORT ON CAMPUS

The types of support you receive will depend on the college you choose, and colleges differ in the programs and support they provide. Your college campus will be unfamiliar terrain to you at first. While entering a new environment will be exciting, you may initially need some guidance. The kinds of support you want to start thinking about in this exercise include:

Academic support. These are the people and centers you can go to get the support you need. From students to faculty to librarians, you can get the help you need from:

- **Subject tutors**
- **A writing center** offers tutors who can help you revise and proofread your papers before submitting them
- **Time-management tutors** help you plan your work and organize your schedule so that you can accomplish all your tasks
- **Professors** or teaching assistants (TAS) clarify material you don't understand
- **Deans and advisors** can help you if you have a problem in your personal life that is interfering with your

work, and they can also help you choose your classes and your major

- **ADD coaches** can help you structure your work and extracurricular tasks and share strategies that have worked for other students with ADD

- **Note-takers** are other students who take notes in class

- **Study groups** can help, as each person in the group prepares a study guide for part of the material and then shares it with the other members of the group

HEADS UP ▉ The most important part of getting the most out of these accommodations is working closely with your professors, deans, advisors, tutors, and anyone else helping you. Don't hesitate to contact deans and advisors as you enter your first semester. You will usually have an academic advisor assigned to you. They help you choose your courses and help you take on any issues you might have in getting your accommodations.

Academic accommodations. The student disabilities services at the college you ultimately choose can give you a full list of the accommodations you are eligible for. They range from special software to early registration for classes. Here are just a few accommodations that you might consider in college:

- extra time for exams (50% or 100%)
- early registration for courses
- use of computers in exams
- use of calculators for exams
- "scribes" (people who write what you dictate to them on tests)
- books on tape

LIFE SKILLS FOR COLLEGE

Do your parents do your laundry? If so, now is the time for you to get a trial run doing your own laundry before heading to campus. Be sure to write down the instructions if you think you'll forget them, and get the proper supplies (including a good laundry bag). Do your parents make all your meals? If you need to figure out how to cook, ask them for a few basic recipes and write them down in your planner, smart phone, or other electronic device. In addition, do your parents

- Help you with your homework?
- Remind you to take things (gym clothes, papers, school supplies) to school?
- Pay your cell phone bill on time?
- Organize your schedule?
- Make your doctor's appointments?
- Make sure you take your medication?

Before you head off to college, identify everything you're going to have to do on your own next year. Make a list of all the tasks someone else (your parents, grandparents, friends, siblings, teachers, tutors, etc.) does for you. Keep all these things in mind as you compile a list of the support you need at college. And, oh yeah, try to thank your parents before you leave for college!

- e-book readers
- text-to-speech or speech-to-text software

Foreign language waivers. Not all colleges grant foreign language waivers, even if you've received one in high school. If foreign languages are difficult for you, think about how important to you an exemption from studying a foreign language in college is—before you apply to college. While you don't want to make this the only criterion for applying to college, you should make it a factor if having a foreign language waiver is a critical issue for you. Note that some colleges only require you to take a class in another culture (not a foreign language), and other schools have creative options for fulfilling your language requirement, such as taking a class in American Sign Language.

Other support you might need. Not only will you need academic support in college, you also might need medical help or help from an RA (resident advisor—an older student or faculty member who oversees the dorms) if you have roommate issues. You might even need some support when you're feeling overwhelmed by school or just need someone, like a therapist or counselor, to talk to if you're going through a tough time with personal stuff. Here's a brief rundown of other kinds of support you may need outside of class:

- counseling support
- gym facilities
- medical facilities
- single dorm rooms
- RA in your dorm

Now that we've gone over the general kinds of support you'll find in college, it's your turn to evaluate which types of support are most critical to you and which you can and cannot live without. Rank the support you'll need below in order of greatest to least importance. File this away in your portfolio or make a spreadsheet—find a way to keep track of this information. You will need to refer to these criteria when you start researching colleges. Refer to these criteria when you are creating your list of priorities for what you are looking for in a college *and* when you visit colleges.

The most critical support/accomodations I need for college:

1. _____

2. _____

3. _____

4. _____

5. _____

Other kinds of support/accommodations that are less important:

1. _____

2. _____

3. _____

4. _____

5. _____

CHAPTER 2

YOUR TRANSCRIPT & GPA

There are a lot of elements that go into preparing your applications to college. Your transcript—the courses you've taken in high school and the grades you've received—is the most important part of your application. To get your transcript to be college-application-ready, take a good look at the courses you are taking. While all four years of high school are important, your junior year is probably the most important, so take your time choosing the right courses during this critical year. You will apply to college with only the first half of your senior year grades, so colleges will take a good look at your junior year grades. Most high schools offer advanced or AP courses during your junior and senior years. You can begin to distinguish yourself in the area you like best—whether it's math, English, science, history, or art—during your junior year.

Work closely with your college counselor (if your school has one) or guidance counselor, advisor, and your parents as you select your courses. If you work with an ADD coach or a tutor, also talk to them about your course selection. These people know your learning style—and your academic strengths and weaknesses—and can help you build the strongest transcript to present to colleges.

As you choose courses, here are some pointers as you start looking at your transcript and selecting courses for your junior year.

- **Aim for a balance** of difficult classes and those you know you can do well in. For example, you might take some advanced classes, but don't take them merely to have them on your transcript.

- **Be realistic and honest** about how much work advanced classes will take. While you want to stretch yourself academically and work up to your potential, don't load yourself down with too many difficult courses that play to your weaknesses. For example, consider whether they give too much reading each night or focus only on test-taking rather than on projects.

- **Save time for classes you enjoy to avoid burnout.** If you overburden yourself, you won't likely earn top grades and may feel burned out. And you might even end up hating school.

- **Take summer school classes** if you have to make up missing work or improve poor grades or skills. Summer classes can help you better the skills you identified as weak in your SWOT analysis. For example, the summer can be an ideal time to work on your writing or build on your missing math skills before taking much more difficult classes in your junior and/or senior years.

Finessing your transcript can be challenging, which is why getting help from others for this task is so important. Your teachers, college counselor, and your parents can help you create a balanced transcript that showcases your strengths, challenges you, and makes you look good to the colleges you'll apply to.

And remember, lots of students with ADD or LD show

great academic improvement as they move through high school. In other words, your grades from freshman year might not be so hot, whereas you might have excelled in your junior year classes. (This is a good thing—and you should point to it in supplements to your application.) Here are a few examples of ways in which you can show improvement over the course of your years in high school:

- **You can show improvement by earning all As and Bs in your junior and senior years,** if you mainly had Bs and the occasional C in your ninth grade and 10th grade years.

- **You can show steady progress by moving from introductory science, math, and history classes to the advanced classes you feel comfortable taking,** such as advanced biology, calculus, or advanced history.

- **You can take summer school classes, attend workshops, and go to camps** to supplement your strong classes or extracurriculars or to improve your skills in your weaker classes.

CHAPTER 3

YOUR EXTRACURRICULARS

Extracurriculars are a great way for students with non-traditional learning profiles to build on their strengths. Admissions officers are looking for students to round out their campus life, and they will consider which ways you can add to the school. While your extracurricular activities can't necessarily make up for low grades, they round out your profile and make you stand out to college admissions committees.

Extracurricular activities also offer experiences that aren't cookie-cutter or one-size-fits-all. You may have problems in math but really enjoy building stage sets or playing soccer. Students with ADD or LD tend to be very creative, and work outside the classroom—whether on the athletic field, artists' studio, or concert hall—allows their talents to shine. Extracurriculars are a critical part of your portfolio, and colleges will ask you about them on your application. Outside interests also provide you with interesting material to write about on your college application essay and to talk about in your college interview. (You'll find out more about the essay and interview process later.)

As early as your sophomore year, take a look at your extracurricular activities. If you aren't involved in any, you should definitely start building up this part of your portfolio as soon as possible. But remember, do these activities for you—enjoy them! They're a great way to find out what you like, who you are, and make friends. By your senior year, you should consider taking on leadership roles in the clubs or activities you belong to, such as serving on a committee for student government or heading up a fundraiser for a club.

- **If you're an artist,** get involved in building stage sets for the school play or take lessons at your community center or local art institute (if there is one). Be sure to save the pieces of studio art you produce or take pictures of your designs to make them part of your college application portfolio.

- **If you are a musician,** join the school band or start your own rock band. Take lessons from a local instructor or join the local symphony if you're a classical musician. Become an instructor and give lessons.

- **Interested in politics?** Join student government or the debate team.

- **Like helping others?** Get involved in community service or volunteering at your favorite animal shelter. Volunteer with local groups in your community in an area or field that interests you.

- **Build on your interest in sports.** For example, if you're a soccer player, consider joining a club team or league outside of your high school team.

- **If you are very busy during the school year,** consider taking on a summer class or internship that builds on your talents. Attend camps or workshops that focus on your interests.

In other words, be sure that you can show colleges how your extracurricular talents have contributed to your school career and how you might build on these activities in college.

CHAPTER 4

STANDARDIZED TESTS

Many students take their first PSAT in their sophomore year so they can have a good read on how they are testing. Keep in mind that many students' scores go up by the time they re-take their PSAT in the fall of their junior year. If students first take the PSAT in the fall of their junior year, their scores often climb by the time they take the SAT in the winter or spring of their junior year. This boost in scores is generally because students have been exposed to additional reading and math material from the time of their first PSAT to the time of their next test. It can help to make yourself a complete timeline for taking these tests.

STANDARDIZED TEST TIMELINE
JUNIOR YEAR

Summer Before	• Decide whether to take the SAT or ACT
	• Make sure your accommodations on the SAT or ACT are in order
	• Start preparing for the SAT or ACT
Winter/ Spring	• Take the SAT or ACT
	• Take Subject Tests and AP exams
	• Assess your scores

SENIOR YEAR

Fall	• Retake the SAT or ACT (if you need to)
	• Possibly take remaining Subject Tests

HEADS UP ! You may want to push your testing as late as possible in your high school career to give yourself as much exposure to math as you can. Check the College Board (which administers the SAT) and ACT websites to see the math topics covered on each test. If you haven't yet taken all the math that's covered on the test until junior year, you may want to take your tests at the end of your junior year or the beginning of your senior year. Talk to your college guidance counselor about your options and the timing of your tests.

Need-to-Know Test Info

Even before you decide which test you're going to take, it's important to get a good lay of the land when it comes to your tests and test scores. Do you have to take standardized tests to get into college? Can you choose your scores? This section will answer these questions.

ARE SOME TESTS OPTIONAL?

Many students are convinced that they have to earn perfect or near-perfect scores on the SAT or ACT to get into the college of their dreams. Yes, some of the most selective colleges and universities use these tests as a way to screen out some applicants (after all, these colleges reject a great deal of their applicant pool). However, more and more colleges, including some very competitive schools, are not requiring the SAT or ACT for admissions. The National Center for Fair & Open Testing maintains a list of these schools, so be sure to check it out on their website (www.fairtest.org/university/optional).

CAN I CHOOSE THE SCORES TO SEND TO COLLEGES?

If you take an exam more than once, the College Board

and the ACT let you choose which scores to send to colleges. These policies (called Score Choice™ for the SAT) mean that, theoretically, you can sit for a test for practice even if you don't want to report the scores to colleges. This option allows you to get more familiar with testing under actual conditions. But keep in mind that you must pay for each test administration you take, and the cost of taking these tests can add up.

HEADS UP Some colleges may not accept Score Choice™. They may require you to submit all your scores. Be sure to check the policies of the colleges you are interested in applying to first. Also, verify that these policies are still in effect with the College Board and ACT, as these options may change in the future. You can find a list of colleges' and scholarships' requirements and policies on the College Board website.

As you can see, there's a lot to consider when it comes to standardized tests. Follow this checklist to keep track of what you'll need to do.

TESTING CHECKLIST

☐ Decide which test to take

☐ Request accommodations

☐ Prepare for the SAT or ACT

☐ Take the test!

A good way to go about setting yourself up for success on standardized tests is to take a measured approach and use the checklist above as a guide. Then you can add your SAT or ACT scores to your portfolio.

Decide Which Test to Take

There are some key differences between the SAT and the ACT. You should understand the differences and choose the test that you think plays to your strengths. A very important consideration to keep in mind about these tests is that the ACT tends to test more knowledge that you've learned in school, while many argue that the SAT seems to test how well you know the test itself rather than a specific area of study. Here's a table that gives you a quick comparison of the two tests:

SAT v. ACT: THE BASICS

	SAT	ACT
Accepted by?	Most colleges	Most colleges
Focus of test	Critical thinking and problem solving	What a student has learned in school
Main skills tested	Vocabulary Grammar Critical reading Math	Grammar Critical reading Math Scientific reasoning
Penalty for wrong answers?	Yes	No
Test structure	Math Critical reading Writing Experimental *(either verbal or math, not clear if it's experimental)*	Math Reading English Science Experimental *(clearly marked as experimental)*
Writing section	Mandatory	Optional
Math coverage	about 50% of test	25% of test
Length	3 hours 45 minutes *(with regular time conditions)*	3 hours *(without writing portion)*

Choosing whether the ACT or SAT is better for you depends upon your preferred learning style and how you study best. Here's a comparison of the SAT and ACT with regard to learning issues:

SAT v. ACT: IF YOU HAVE ADD OR LD

	SAT	ACT
Math LD	Better for students who do well in math	Better for students with math disorders, as it has less math (but some of the math is more advanced)
Writing LD	Better for students who write well under pressure	Better for students who struggle with writing, as the essay is optional
ADD	Consider applying for multiple-day testing, as the test is very long	Consider applying for multiple-day testing, but the test isn't as long without the writing section

Using this information, you can decide which test is best for you. Now you have to request accommodations, register, and study.

Request Accommodations

The SAT or ACT both offer accommodations. Because they are administered by separate organizations, they may have (slightly) different accommodations available and may require different types of documentation. The types of accommodations that are available include:

- 50% or 100% extended time (Keep in mind that extra-time accommodations will make the tests quite long. Be sure to practice taking entire tests with extra time before the test day to get used to sitting and concentrating for hours on end.)

- testing over multiple days
- frequent and/or longer breaks
- small group setting or a private room
- computer use for writing the essays
- many other accommodations

To apply for these accommodations, you (usually) must have an evaluation by a qualified professional, such as a psychologist or neuropsychologist, that was conducted within the last three to five years. This evaluation must document your need for accommodations and back up this need with testing. As stated above, each testing organization has different requirements, so be sure to consult these websites and your college guidance counselor about getting your documentation in order to apply for accommodations well in advance of the tests. Remember that just because you request these accommodations, you may not receive them.

Prepare for the SAT or ACT

After you take the PSAT, you should come up with a plan about how you are going to prepare for the SAT or ACT. There are many ways to prepare. Generally, just taking the test again and again under timed conditions and familiarizing yourself with the different sections of the test will help you boost your scores. Come up with a timeline, like the one in the beginning of the chapter, to help you get organized for your test prep.

Just looking at a test-prep timeline might seem a little overwhelming, as you have school, college applications, and your life to handle as well! But keep in mind that the most important part of your college application portfolio is your grades. Don't spend so much time preparing for standardized tests that you let your schoolwork—or your basic well-being—slide. You want to plan ahead and pace your studying over a few months so that you don't try to cram right before the tests or harm your school performance.

Below are some ways students prepare—some students use a combination of these methods, while some just use one. How you prepare depends on how much time you want to spend studying for the standardized tests, what your (and your family's) budget allows, and how important the scores are for your overall college application portfolio.

- **Check whether your high school offers a test-prep course.** If it does, register! Many high schools offer test-prep courses at a reduced rate.

- **Take professional review courses or hire private tutors** to help you prepare for the tests. These can be expensive, so before taking this step, consider how important the SAT or ACT is to your college admissions portfolio. For example, if you are considering applying to a school that makes the ACT or SAT optional, you may not need to spend a great deal of time on preparation.

- **Prepare for the tests on your own.** Familiarize yourself with each part of the test and order practice tests from the College Board and from the ACT. Each organization offers some free tests online.

- **Buy test-prep guides** that teach you test-taking strategies and that offer sample exams with the explanation of each answer.

- **Read books, magazines, and newspapers** that contain the types of material that the tests ask you to analyze. These include passages related to literature, humanities, social sciences (history, economics, sociology, etc.), and science.

Prepare for Subject Tests

More tests?! Yes, you'll have to consider which other tests you have to take to apply to the colleges you're interested in. Some colleges require two (or even three) SAT Subject Tests, also administered by the College Board. Be sure to check which tests—there are 20 from which you can choose—you will need to take. Also make note of the deadlines for submitting your scores. Now's a good time to speak with your guidance counselor about which you should take. As you're taking a look at Subject Tests, here is some helpful information:

- **The easier Subject Tests are those taken by a wide number of students,** such as U.S. History or Biology, generally speaking. The tests taken by students with a strong science background, such as Physics or Chemistry, tend to be more difficult as they are scored with a different curve.

- **Be sure to take the tests that you will do well on** and that are tailored to your interests in college.

- **It might be easiest to take the Subject Tests related to the advanced or AP classes you've taken,** as you will most likely be prepared for these tests. Check the College Board website for the timing of these tests.

- **You can begin to take Subject Tests in your sophomore year** (or even freshman year if you've

GET READING!

A good way to get ready for the reading sections—not to mention to be prepared for the reading you will be required to do in college—is to read high-quality publications, such as *The New Yorker*, *The Atlantic*, or *The Economist*. Check out the science section of a newspaper, such as *The New York Times*, *The Washington Post*, or *The Los Angeles Times*. There are also plenty of online publications like *Slate*, *Salon*, or *The Huffington Post*. Write down all the unfamiliar vocabulary you encounter on flash cards, and keep reviewing these words. This type of preparation will also help you to be a more fluent reader.

taken an applicable course such as biology) and throughout your junior year and into the fall of your senior year.

Now that you've begun to build your portfolio, you can embark on the more enjoyable part of the process—exploring colleges that are a good fit for you and your interests.

JUNIOR YEAR:
SPRING-SUMMER

FINDING THE RIGHT COLLEGE FOR YOU

A huge part of the college application process is identifying schools that are right for you. Don't believe that college X—whether it's Florida State or Northwestern; your local community college; the school where your parents, brother, or girlfriend or boyfriend went; or what's ranked as the nation's number one party school—is the best school for you without really checking it out. After all, you are a unique individual, and you need a school that's right for you—one that will enhance and develop your strengths, help you steer around your weaknesses or compensate for them, make you feel good about yourself, and launch you into a meaningful career, hopefully without saddling you with unbearable debt.

Once you know what you need and want in a college, finding the right match is going to be a whole lot easier for you. Right now, choosing from among the thousands of colleges and universities in the United States may appear staggeringly complicated because you haven't yet decided what you're looking for. Finding the right college involves a few steps.

Here's what you'll need to do:

- First, you need to decide what you want in a college.

- Then, you need look at schools and get an idea whether they are right for you.

- As you're completing this process, you'll have your notebook or laptop at the ready so you can record if schools are a good fit for your needs, academic record, and abilities.

Let's get started.

CHAPTER 5

PREPARE TO RESEARCH

It's easy to fall prey to believing what other people tell you about colleges, but you can't possibly know where you want to go before you do some research on your own. This isn't the kind of research you do in history class. Instead, it's an interactive kind of research. You will be visiting colleges, asking college students and administrators questions, and picturing your future life beyond high school. This is interesting investigative work that has YOU at its center.

Here are some of the considerations you should keep in mind as you begin to do your research:

- Do I want to move or stay close to home?
- Do I want a big school or a tiny one?
- What's my family's budget?
- Do I care about college ranking websites or magazines?
- Do I want to go to a two- or four-year school?
- What kinds of accommodations do I need at college?

All of this information, considered together, will help you figure out what you want in a school.

HEADS UP Be sure to show the list of your college priorities to your parents, especially if they will be paying for college. You need their agreement on your top priorities for choosing a school, and this process should be a negotiation between you and your parents about what you want and need and what they are willing to agree to. You may or may not enjoy this discussion, but remember that it's better for you to hash out an agreement with your parents at this stage of the process than to find out that you disagree with them once you already have your heart set on a specific school.

Before you dive into this assessment to figure out what kind of school you're looking for, though, let's look at—in detail—a few of the criteria.

CLOSE TO HOME V. FAR FROM HOME

This choice may depend on where you live now. Do you want to live near or far away from your family? Can you afford to travel home if you attend school far away? Are you ready to see a different part of the country, or do you need your family's support? These are important considerations in deciding on the location of your school.

BIG SCHOOLS V. SMALL SCHOOLS

Though there is a great deal of variety among big and small schools, in general universities are larger because they also include graduate schools. Here are some other key differences:

- **At universities, classes tend to be large**—particularly at the introductory level—and can include several hundred students.

- **In large classes, the grading and the instruction of weekly discussion sections are often carried out by teaching assistants,** who are generally graduate students. Therefore, undergraduate students may have little direct contact with their professors.

- **Larger schools can offer a broader range of students** and a great deal of on-campus activities.

- **Smaller schools are usually colleges that don't have**

graduate students. Classes are generally smaller in size, and there are more opportunities for one-on-one time with professors.

- **Smaller schools may have a more limited campus life,** though they can offer a closer-knit community in which students and faculty know each other.

FAMILY BUDGET

Speak with your parents about the financial considerations involved in attending college as early in this process as possible. Be sure to consult with your college guidance counselor, as well, about the types of financial aid available and how to apply for them.

Keep in mind that while the in-state tuition at public colleges is much less than the tuition at most private colleges, out-of-state tuition at public colleges can be a lot more money, though not necessarily as much as the tuition at private schools. Bottom line: check the prices before deciding whether a public or private college is right for you. The location of your school will also affect the cost. If you have to travel a far distance to and from your campus, the cost of attending college will be greater.

SCHOOL RANKINGS

You should not prioritize schools just based on their rankings in the yearly guides about the nation's "best" schools. Though some students select the colleges they want to apply to primarily based on rankings, you should be aware of how these rankings are devised. Remember, just because a school is designated as the "best," it doesn't necessarily mean it's the best for you. "Best" is a generic term that has little relevance to the college that will provide the optimal experience, skills, and education for you. As you read the college rankings, keep the following in mind:

- **The top schools tend to be those that reject the greatest number of applicants.**

- **The rankings of the schools are also based on the opinions of college administrators** and faculty around the country, the number of students who graduate from that college within four years, the standardized test scores and grades of admitted students, the teacher-faculty ratio, and other data.

- **Though these criteria are important, they are generic in nature** and don't really speak to whether a certain college will be a good fit for you and help you develop.

The top schools in the rankings may be good matches for you, but be sure to do a little more digging (this book will help you explore more) before you apply. If they are right for you, by all means apply!

TWO-YEAR SCHOOLS V. FOUR-YEAR SCHOOLS

A big question you might be asking yourself is *What if I don't want to go to a four-year school?* Or *What if I don't get into any four-year schools? What then?* Two-year (or junior) colleges are great places for students who need to bolster their skills.

- **These colleges are nurturing places** for the high school graduate who wants to attend college but who may not be ready for four-year college work yet or who is just not quite sure what to study.

- **They offer skills courses and basic work** that allow students to improve their skills and work habits.

COLLEGE RANKINGS REALITIES

MYTH: Going to a highly ranked school will automatically make you a great success in life.

REALITY: A recent study found that students who had been admitted to prestigious colleges but had instead decided to attend other colleges were AS SUCCESSFUL as their counterparts who had gone to prestigious schools. The researchers determined that what had made the students successful were their inherent qualities, not anything that came from their colleges. You make your future—your school doesn't make it for you.

MYTH: The CEOs and leaders of most major organizations graduated from high-ranking colleges.

REALITY: A recent study of top CEOs found that most of them had attended public colleges and universities, not prestigious colleges.

- **The professors at these schools tend to be very involved** in helping students, giving them lots of one-on-one attention.

- **Students can sometimes transfer to a four-year college** or enter the workforce at the end of a two-year course of study.

- **Two-year community colleges are much less expensive** than four-year colleges and offer you the chance to study close to home.

Going to a community college doesn't mean that you can't eventually graduate from a four-year school (and you'll have better skills and potentially less debt at the end of four years as well!).

ACCOMMODATIONS

There are three general classes of accommodation programs schools can offer. These programs vary with regard to the types of accommodations they offer and the depth of resources they provide to students. Let's take a look at each type of program:

- **Basic accommodations.** Like the name indicates, these are the least robust accommodation programs. Students must request accommodations at schools that offer these programs. These programs' services include extended time or laptop use on tests, but these schools do not have specialized programs for students with ADD or LD.

- **Coordinated programs.** These schools' programs are more extensive than basic programs, but, generally, students must request accommodations in order to receive them. In coordinated programs, there is a director who knows about ADD and LD, and these programs offer accommodations, such as the help of a learning specialist and tutors. These programs also help students advocate for themselves with professors.

- **Structured programs.** These programs provide the most extensive support and are staffed by people who know about ADD and LD. Students enroll directly in these programs, and these programs offer assistance, such as changes in the curriculum and academic counseling and support.

Develop Your College Criteria

Now you will develop the criteria you are looking for in a college. Here's how to use the assessment below in which you will choose your college criteria.

- Make a copy of the assessment, or create your own on your home computer.

- Select the best answer or answers for each question.

- If you don't yet know what you want, check "unsure" and return to that question later, perhaps with the help of a guidance counselor, parent, or teacher.

- When you're finished, prioritize the five criteria that are the most important to you. (After all, you may not to be able to get everything you want in one college, but you may fall in love with the right school anyway.)

- Return to this assessment as you do your research and visit schools. You'll most likely make adjustments to your preferences and your priorities. Nothing is etched in stone!

For each item below, choose what you are looking for in a college. Let's begin!

Your College Criteria

1. Type of school:
   - ☐ a two-year college
   - ☐ a four-year college
   - ☐ unsure

2. School size:
   - ☐ a small college (fewer than 4,000 students)
   - ☐ a mid-size school (about 4,000–10,000 students)
   - ☐ a very large school (thousands of undergraduates and/or graduate students)
   - ☐ unsure

3. **Average class size:**

    ☐ huge, lots of TAs (150–250+ students)

    ☐ medium (75–150 students)

    ☐ small (12–20 students)

    ☐ don't care

    ☐ unsure

4. **Public or private school:**

    ☐ a private college

    ☐ a public college

    ☐ unsure

    ☐ don't care

5. **Financial considerations:**

    ☐ no financial aid

    ☐ some financial aid and/or work-study or other programs

    ☐ cost is an important consideration for me and my family

6. **School setting:**

    ☐ a large urban area with a great deal to do off campus

    ☐ a small town that is centered around the campus

    ☐ unsure

7. **Regional location (check all that apply):**

    ☐ the Northeast/Mid-Atlantic

    ☐ the West

    ☐ the South

    ☐ the Midwest

    ☐ unsure

    ☐ don't care

8. **Academic scope:**

☐ many majors

☐ a specific major or specialized program, such as business, art, or music

if so, specify your interest here: _____

9. **Social climate:**

☐ a liberal school

☐ an ideologically conservative school

☐ a school of a specific religious or racial background or a single-sex school

if so, specify your interest here: _____

☐ unsure

☐ don't care

10. **Accommodations:**

☐ basic accommodations

☐ coordinated programs

☐ structured programs

☐ other support/accommodations

11. **Other programs (check all that apply):**

☐ sports

specify sport and level here: _____

☐ clubs

specify sport and level here: _____

☐ other extracurricular activities

specify sport and level here: _____

☐ work programs/co-ops

12. Housing and dorm options (check all that apply):

☐ single rooms

☐ single-sex dorms

☐ co-ed dorms

☐ off-campus housing

☐ sorority/fraternity house

☐ live at home

☐ don't care

13. Diversity of the student body:

☐ very diverse, a total melting pot

☐ some diversity, but not everyone is represented

☐ homogenous

☐ don't care

14. Other considerations (faculty with a particular expertise, study abroad programs, etc.):

_____

_____

_____

_____

_____

HEY, WAIT! WHAT'S NOT ON THIS LIST?

You probably noticed that the questions about figuring out your criteria for choosing a college didn't
include the following:

- **Which schools have the hottest guys/girls.** Yes,
  there are websites you can go to for this information. You may have even visited them. But it seems
  pretty subjective and is not the best way to pick
  a school. You will find the best friends and more-
  than-friends at the school that's right for you in
  other ways.

- **Which are the best party schools.** If this is a very
  important priority for you, you may want to examine why you are choosing to go to college in the
  first place. Do you really want to spend a lot of
  your parents' money and/or loan money that you
  will be working to pay off for years on partying?
  No, this doesn't mean that you can't enjoy the
  social scene at your school, but hedonistic partying shouldn't be your top priority. School can
  cost a lot of money, and it's the ticket to your
  future work and intellectual life. If all you want to
  do is party in college, consider taking a year off to
  explore your options.

- **Which have the best sports teams.** Though you
  may follow a well-known college sports team,
  you may not like these schools outside the football stadium. Schools with big-time athletics may
  not offer you the types of support or programs
  you need to be successful. You can still watch
  your favorite team without committing yourself to
  attending its school.

Use Your Criteria

Now that you know your criteria for choosing a college from the list above, take a good look at your selections. As you do so, ask yourself what the most important considerations are to you in a college. Then, rank your top five criteria. (If you have problems doing this, talk to your parents, your college guidance counselor, or a teacher.) This list will be your main guide as you research schools, as you'll see how each college measures up to your priorities. You will use these criteria as you take college tours, attend college talks and fairs, and read about colleges to figure out the schools that make your final list of colleges you'd like to apply to.

Prioritize Your Criteria

1. _____

2. _____

3. _____

4. _____

5. _____

DEVELOP A LIST OF SCHOOLS

Now that you have a list of the most important criteria to look for in a school, you are ready to come up with potential colleges. You can certainly research that school you've always dreamed about—whether it's your state school or the school your grandfather attended—and figure out if it fits your criteria. However, be very wary of changing your criteria to fit a school simply based on its reputation and ranking. Keep an open mind! You might be surprised by which schools make your list and which don't.

HEADS UP While you want to include some reaches among your schools, you need to be realistic. Don't think that just because you want to get into a school that you will. A lot of students think that their glowing personalities will make up for less-than-stellar academic records or less-than-desirable standardized test scores. Be sure that your grades and scores meet at least the minimum requirements for that school.

Now begin. With your criteria in hand, start gathering info. To find a list of schools that meet your criteria, you'll probably want to use some, if not all, of the following sources:

- **The college guidance counselor** at your school (if there is one).

- **The College Board** (www.collegeboard.com) has a handy search tool. On this website, you can enter different criteria, which you have already figured out from the questionnaire above, to find some schools that might be a good match for you.

- **A general guide to colleges.** Your school guidance counselor, or local or school library might have some of these guides, so you may not need to purchase them.

- **A guide specific to colleges** with services for students with learning disabilities.

- **Brochures and pamphlets** that you receive in the mail or via e-mail.

- **College fairs.**

- **People you know**—graduates of your school, older friends, siblings, and others—who went to certain colleges. You can speak with these students to find out more information about their colleges and whether they'd be the right fit for you. Don't feel shy about approaching people for help. People generally love speaking about the schools they attended and their college experiences.

- **Teachers** usually know which colleges offer solid programs in their area of study, and they can also help you find graduates of your school who attended certain colleges. If, for example, you want to major in art, start by asking your art teacher about the schools he or she attended. Remember that they went through the process as well and that they are eager to help people who show an interest in their field.

Using Your Priority List

As you find schools that look like a fit, put them to the test. How many of your priorities does the school have? How well does it match your priority list?

Throughout the process, keep your top five priorities

in mind. There are certain things you simply can't live without. Use your priorities list as you look at schools. Make sure you're sticking to what you've decided are the most important criteria you want and need in a school. For example, if you know you are a city person and can't attend a rural college, it doesn't matter if your friend loves attending school in rural Minnesota—that school simply isn't for you. If you are really interested in a certain program—such as undergraduate business or art—don't apply to a school, no matter how prestigious or well-recommended, if it doesn't have this program.

However, while you may have to be a bit flexible about some of your less important priorities, be sure to keep your most critical criteria in mind and objectively examine whether each school you explore meets these criteria.

Once you have a list pulled together, take a second closer look. Does it have a mix of colleges on this list? Do you have some reaches—schools that will be difficult for you to get into? Some solid choices—schools you think you have an acceptable chance of getting into? What about some "safety schools" for which you far exceed the entry requirements? Do you have at least 10 schools (and most likely many more) potential colleges on this list? Have you kept an open mind? Don't forget, looking at a school and putting it on your list doesn't mean you have to apply to it.

Now you have your preliminary list. You should meet with your college guidance counselor about how realistic and comprehensive your list is. Also, consider it a changeable list—add and subtract schools as needed. Make it as long as you need to. Later on in the search process, you will compose another list of solid college choices after you've researched the schools further by visiting campuses, speaking with students, and consulting your college guidance counselor and parents.

Try to enjoy this process and have fun! Remember, just as you did with your priority list:

- **Make a copy of the list,** or create your own on your home computer.

- **Return to it as you do your research and visit schools.** This list will, more likely than not, change as you visit schools and do more research.

My First List of Potential Colleges

Reaches

1. _____

2. _____

3. _____

4. _____

Solid Choices

1. _____

2. _____

3. _____

4. _____

Safety Schools

1. _____

2. _____

3. _____

4. _____

You have your list of potential colleges. It's time to check them out—in person!

CHAPTER 7

TOuR COLLEGES

Now that you have your first list of potential colleges, you have to dig deeper and find out if they're a good fit for you. One of the best ways to do this type of research—in addition to reading the colleges' websites—is to contact the colleges to arrange tours. This is the fun part.

HEADS UP ▌ Colleges are wary of "stealth applicants" who suddenly submit an application without having had any previous contact with the school. So, if you can't manage to tour a college in person, call the admissions office. Or at least register for e-mail updates or sign up to be on their mailing list to show that you are seriously interested in that school. Your finances may not allow you to visit each and every college on your list, but you may be able to visit your serious choices.

Here are some tips to keep in mind as you start planning for tours:

- **Try to visit colleges when you will get a good sense of what they're like.** Touring colleges during the summer won't give you the best idea of what it would be like to attend them because many students aren't on campus and most classes aren't in session. (The same is true of spring and winter breaks.)

- **Take advantage of virtual tours.** Go online and see what kind of tours they have posted.

- **Call the admissions office for information.** Some

schools track any kind of communication (points of contact) a student has had with the college, even if the student can't visit in person.

- **Participate in live chats with admissions staff.** Some schools host dedicated chat times, when you can ask questions of staff and current students in real time.

- **Tour a local or regional college** that you aren't necessarily going to apply to before you tour the schools you're really interested in. This practice tour will help you get a better sense of what to expect and what kinds of questions to ask on your real tours.

- **Visit the school's Facebook and other social networking pages.**

- **Combine trips to colleges to reduce expenses.** If you have a bunch of schools in the Boston area, make it a point to visit all of those on your list in one weekend.

- **Seek out local alternatives.** Many colleges also travel to local fairs and host information sessions at high schools. These types of local events can be a good alternative to visiting if you can't make it to campus.

HEADS UP ! When you are touring schools, make yourself an active participant in the process. Attend class and, if possible, stay overnight in the dorms. You can contact colleges to help you set up overnight visits. While your parents can go with you, don't allow them to ask all the questions. Remember, you are going to be the one attending the school, and you have to be part of the process of finding the right college.

TourGanization

To stay organized, make a chart or spreadsheet that tracks your progress during the process of contacting colleges to arrange tours. Take a look at an example of how to set one up.

COLLEGE TOURS

School	Jane Doe U.	
Date Contacted		
Tour Date and Time		
Interview Date and Time		
Important Contacts		

You can make a chart for each tour, too.

JANE DOE U. TOUR

Travel Itinerary		
Hotel Info		
Admissions Contact		
Tour Date and Time		

Touring With ADD and LD

When you're visiting colleges, keep in mind how you best collect and organize information, given your learning style. Here are some pointers:

If you are a **visual learner**,

- **Take pictures** to remind yourself of what the college really looks like, particularly if you are touring a bunch of schools.

- **Take a short set of notes** at each school to record your observations accurately for later reference.

- **Collect literature from the college admissions office** to remind you what you saw on your visit.

If you have a **non-verbal learning disability (NLD)** and tend to want to avoid new social experiences,

- **Travel with a good friend** from high school or a close relative.

- **Stay with a family friend** or a graduate of your school—perhaps an outgoing person—who can smooth the way for you a bit at first.

- **Submit questions via e-mail or online chats** if you feel uncomfortable asking questions on the tour.

If you have **ADD** and have a hard time sitting through presentations, tours, and the like,

- **Bring a pad and paper or smartphone with you on the tours.** Write down your questions and take notes on the answers.

- **Check out the schools' websites** for more lively, interactive information

OTHER WAYS TO RESEARCH COLLEGES

Even if you can't visit each and every college you apply to, you can still research that school thoroughly. Good ways to get to know a school are the following:

- **Speak to alumni**, and not necessarily only the person who interviews you (if you have an alumni interviewer). You can find alumni through the college or through people who attended your high school and went to the college you are interested in. Ask your college guidance counselor about alumni of a particular college who attended your high school.

- **Speak to current students.** You can get their names from alumni who graduated from your high school, from parents and friends, or from the college itself.

- **Read the college's newspaper and other publications.** Keep in mind that the video and catalogue the colleges put out aren't likely to be as objective or insightful about the true tenor of campus life as student-written publications are.

- **If you're an athlete, speak to current members of the school's team** about what it's really like to play at that school.

- **Get off the tour** and, to the extent allowed, explore the college campus on your own. Talk to current students. You're sure to turn up some interesting information.

- **Create an e-mail account** specifically for all the college admissions related messages that you receive.

(Make sure your e-mail handle is appropriate—superburper@e-mail.com does not look good on an application.)

No matter what kind of LD you have, work with your strengths to get the most out of your college tour. And make sure you're an active participant by asking good questions.

Tour & Visit Questions

To determine whether a school is a good match for you, you need to observe the school on the tour and ask questions. As you research schools, remind yourself of the criteria you are looking for in schools—you made that list for a reason! Don't be swayed by a student center with a plasma TV, a library filled with soft couches, or a dining hall with an ice cream sundae bar. Instead, go to the college armed with a list of questions that help you figure out if that school offers what you need. Concentrate on asking questions about the college and students' lives there to break the ice with people you meet. After all, people love to talk about themselves and their experiences.

Below is a list of questions for you to bring on your college tours. Take a look and familiarize yourself with them. Mark the ones that fit your needs, and write them down so you can record the answers on your tours. Feel free to add to or alter the questions depending on the school you're visiting and your specific needs.

Support Systems & Accommodations

1. Do you need to ask whether the colleges offer the following?

    • extended time for testing (50% or 100%)

- subject-matter tutoring
- time-management help
- assistance with choosing courses
- the ability to register first or early for courses
- note-takers
- computer use for tests
- books on tape
- other accommodations

2. **What are the documentation requirements at their school to grant you accommodations?**

3. **If there's a tutoring center, what are the tutors like? Are they fellow students, graduate students, or professors?**

   3a. How do I sign up to see a tutor?

   3b. Which subjects do they tutor in?

   3c. Do they offer classes for first-year students about study skills and dorm life?

   3d. Do they offer time-management classes?

The following questions are good to ask current students or recent grads.

4. **Is it easy to get and use the accommodations I need?**

5. **Is it easy to work with tutors on campus or with professors or deans if I need extra help?**

   5a. How do students work with them?

   In asking about the types of accommodations offered, you don't need to necessarily reveal that you have ADD or LD to the admissions office. You can ask a student, librarian, dean, or the office for students with disabilities about these types of services. You can also search for this information on schools' websites or in their catalogues.

Finances & Tuition

6. **How much do extra services—or accommodations—cost?** (Don't automatically assume that colleges offer these services without any additional cost.)

7. **What percentage of students graduate within four years?** Be wary of schools at which a large percentage of students take longer than four years to graduate. If a large percentage of students—especially those with learning disabilities—don't graduate within four years but take five or six years, you might be facing even greater tuition costs (and debt).

Medical Services

8. **How does the medical system work at this school?**

9. **How do I set up appointments with doctors or counselors, and is it easy to see them?**

10. Are there many doctors on campus who are schooled in my needs (for example, a psychiatrist who has worked with students with ADD or other concerns)?

Library

11. Are there quiet places to study?

12. Are there a lot of computers?

13. Are there facilities for listening to books on tape or other assistive technologies I need?

Gym Facilities & Athletics

14. How easy is it to visit the gym and does it get really crowded?

   14a. Are there good machines to use?

If you're considering playing sports, visit the sports facilities and attend a practice or game.

15. What are the coach and the facilities like?

16. Is there a good chance (no kidding yourself) that I could play on this team?

Dorms & Dining

17. What are the party dorms? What are the quietest dorms?

18. Are there single rooms if I need them?

19. Are there kitchens or other facilities that I need?

20. What are the laundry rooms like? Are they always crowded?

21. Does the dining hall offer food I would really eat?

22. What are current students' favorite dining halls and/or meals?

Classes & Professors

23. How large are the big intro classes? Are the lecture halls packed?

   23a. How engaged do the students seem?

   23b. What are the TAs like? How big are the discussion sections?

24. If you can visit smaller classes, how engaging are the professors?

24a. Do the students participate in class discussions?

School List, Redux

After you've done your research and gone on tours, you might find that the schools you really like have changed. That's good! Here's a chance for you to reflect on everything you've learned about the schools and how closely they match your priorities.

Fill out the revised list of your college choices. Check with your college guidance counselor and parents about

CAN YOU FIND A QUIET PLACE TO STUDY?

Finding where you will study at each potential school is important. On your tours, figure out where you would study in a quiet place. If it's difficult to find such a place, it may be a sign that this college isn't right for you. Are the dorms too chaotic to imagine doing solid work there? Are there secluded places in the library so that you can study in isolation if you need to? Locating these study spots will enable you to go campus for your first year of school having already scouted out a secure work location. Many students who have trouble concentrating find that they also need to use noise-canceling headphones to fully block out distractions while studying in their dorms or in the library. While these headphones are expensive, many students swear by them. Industrial-strength earplugs are a wallet-friendly alternative.

this list to be sure you've included the appropriate range of schools that everyone can agree on.

Reaches

1. _____

2. _____

3. _____

4. _____

Solid Choices

1. _____

2. _____

3. _____

4. _____

Safety Schools

1. _____

2. _____

3. _____

4. _____

Now that you've explored colleges and found a mix of schools you think are good fits for you, you are ready to take the next step—formally applying to the schools and letting them know about you and what you have to offer.

SENIOR YEAR: FALL-WINTER

PUTTING TOGETHER YOUR APPLICATION

This section will help you put together all the elements of your application that you started thinking about during your junior year. Your application uses all the parts of your portfolio—your transcript, your test scores, your teachers' recommendations, and your extracurricular activities. You will use each part of the portfolio in the applications you to send to colleges, and this chapter will lead you through each step of the process.

Students who've gone through the college application process suggest that the earlier you start working on your applications, the better. Planning ahead is essential. Don't leave your application packages to the last minute. Instead, take a look at everything you need to include for your applications and use the tracking sheet below to help you organize yourself. Otherwise, you will be completing your regular-admissions applications just before the end of your first semester of senior year, which is a very busy time. To reduce stress, take a look at the timeline in the beginning of the book to get a sense of what you'll need to do. Then start planning out how you are going to complete each step without it getting overwhelming.

If you aren't good about submitting materials by the deadlines, you will probably need someone, like a parent, to help you. Use the chart on the next page to organize your application deadlines. Post this chart in your room, and enlist someone—a parent, teacher, a tutor—to help you fill it out. This is one time you really want to make sure you are submitting material on time. Feel free to use this chart as a guideline for building your own chart or application calendar that works for your needs and organization style.

APPLICATION TRACKING SHEET

College		
Common Application?		
Supplements		
Decision Type		
Deadline		
SAT/ACT Scores Submitted?		
Other Test Scores Submitted		
Number of Recommendations		
Recommendations Submitted?		
Interview Required?		
Interview Date		
Transcript Submitted?		
FAFSA Application		
Accepted?		
Deposit Deadline		

CHAPTER 8

ORGANIZE YOUR APPLICATION DEADLINES

There are different deadlines by which you can apply to college, and schools offer various options. Some schools have fixed deadlines, while others have "rolling admissions" by which students can submit their applications over the course of their senior year. At colleges that have fixed deadlines for admissions, students can apply either for regular admission or for early admission (or early action). Check out the comparison of your three options.

DECISIONS, DECISIONS
BASIC INFO

EARLY DECISION	EARLY ACTION	REGULAR DECISION
binding—must attend school if accepted	not binding	no restrictions
can't apply early elsewhere	can apply to other schools (except under single-choice early action plans)	no restrictions
can apply regular decision to other schools	can apply regular admission to other schools	no restrictions
response by winter of senior year	response by winter of senior year	response by spring of senior year
nonrefundable deposit often due early	deposit not usually due until late spring	deposit due in late spring

DECISIONS, DECISIONS
STUDENT-TYPE COMPARISON

EARLY DECISION	EARLY ACTION	REGULAR DECISION
good for students with a clear choice of top school	good for students with a clear choice of top schools	better for students with no clear top choice
good for students with strong or consistent academic record	good for students with strong or consistent academic record	better for students who need senior year to build their portfolios and improve their transcripts

If students are accepted in the early decision program, they must withdraw their applications to other schools. Some schools have two early decision deadlines—early decision I and II. Consult the colleges' websites for the deadlines for each type of decision.

HEADS UP ! Some colleges accept the Common Application, available at www.commonapp.org, though they may also require supplemental information. This means that you can fill out one application to apply to several colleges. The Common Application is released over the summer, so check during the summer before your senior year which colleges accept this application and which require separate applications. You can start working on the Common Application before your senior year begins to reduce stress during the busy academic year.

CHAPTER 9

GET RECOMMENDATIONS

One of the most important steps in the application process is asking the right teachers to write you a recommendation letter. The recommendation should build on what you identified as your strengths in your SWOT analysis (remember from your portfolio?). Plan ahead in considering which teachers should write recommendations on your behalf. Follow a handy recommendation timeline.

RECOMMENDATION TIMELINE

SENIOR YEAR

Summer Before	• Think about which teachers (at least two) you are going to ask to write on your behalf
September– October	• Approach teachers to write recommendations • Prepare recommendation forms from applications (online or hard copy) • Prepare materials for teachers to assist their recommendation writing
November– December	• Collect all recommendations and forms from teachers • Mail forms or submit them electronically by the deadlines • If teachers are mailing forms, check that they've arrived on time

So, who should you ask to write recommendations? Here are some good places to start:

- Teachers who've taught you in your junior and/or senior years and who know you well.

- Teachers in whose classes you've done well and whose subject areas you intend to study in college.

- Teachers who advise student groups you're involved in, such as student government, newspaper, or yearbook.

Be sure to ask a teacher before simply assuming he or she will write a letter for you. Remember, give your recommenders plenty of advance notice. Some students also have a supplementary recommendation from a non-academic mentor, such as

- a coach

- the head of a summer internship program

- a religious or community leader

- an adult who knows you well (and who also possibly attended the college you're applying to)

HEADS UP ! Always write thank you notes to your recommenders. And keep them posted on the outcome of your application process.

Help Your Teachers Write About You

It's your job to help your teachers write fully descriptive and persuasive recommendation letters. Don't just drop your recommendation forms on your teachers' desks and walk away. The best recommendation letters result from a dialogue between you and the teachers you've chosen to write about you. Presumably, you chose these teachers because you did fairly well in their classes and they know you. However, they usually have taught you in your junior or senior year and may not know everything about your earlier years in high school. So be sure to let them know the following kinds of information:

- **What obstacles you've faced** and how you've turned weaknesses into strengths in the classroom.

- **Any outside interests you have or leadership roles you've played** that you think will enhance your application profile.

- **Any academic interests that you developed** in the classroom that you've furthered through outside work.

If a teacher can write about how you turned your weaknesses into strengths, you will have a compelling story to tell college admissions officers. For example, a teacher can write about how you were at first disorganized but then worked to develop your own fool-proof organizational system tailored to your needs or about how you worked on your reading skills over the summer by developing your own list of sports-related titles that you devoured. Everyone likes a student who comes from behind to achieve success.

CHAPTER 10

FACE YOUR ESSAY

Writing an essay (or personal statement) that really wows the admissions offices takes a long time. It's a process best completed over time with plenty of room for revision and rethinking. You should start thinking about your personal statement during the summer before your senior year. If you can finish it before your busy senior year starts, you'll be in good shape. Then, over the fall, you can have teachers and your guidance officer read it and provide you with suggestions for revision.

The essay is the most personal—and often the most difficult—piece of the college admissions process. But don't let it scare you. With careful planning and an early start, you'll write an essay that showcases your talents. To some degree, the essay is like salesmanship, and it's difficult to sell yourself or to think about yourself objectively. And you must do so in 500 words or less. The key is to write about yourself in positive, though not arrogant, terms, and to consider yourself honestly.

Think About Your Topic

To write your essay, you must think of a topic that helps colleges understand who you are as a person and why you would be a good fit for their school. You can start the process by asking relatives, friends, teachers, and others what you think sets you apart. Ultimately, though, the essay topic has to come from you. Before you actually write your essay, brainstorm potential topics. As you ponder topics, keep these guidelines in mind:

- **Admissions committees can sniff out insincerity.** Don't write about something that is totally inconsistent with your high school record, your accomplishments and interests, and who you are as a person. Instead, write about something genuine.

- **Try to avoid potentially controversial topics,** such as religion or politics (unless you are applying to the type of school at which this essay speaks to their mission), or at least present these issues in a context that's not polemical.

- **Avoid topics that are likely to anger or disgust your readers.** No brainer.

Here are some questions to ask yourself as you think of potential topics:

- What has been the most formative experience in your life?

- What has contributed the most to your growth as a high school student?

- What do you want the college admissions office to know about you as a person?

- What isn't expressed by your scores or grades that you want college admissions staff to know about (for example, extracurricular activities you are involved with)?

- How has overcoming your ADD or LD helped you come to understand yourself and how your mind works?

COMMON TYPES OF ESSAY QUESTIONS

Along with (or instead of) an open-ended personal statement, some colleges have required questions for you to answer. Here is a brief list of the most common questions:

- Describe yourself and the significant experiences that have formed you.
- What are your educational and career goals?
- Why is our college a good fit for you?
- Describe a person in history or in your life who has had an important effect on you.

Write Your Essay

Now that you've nailed down your essay topic, it's time to start writing. It's best to approach your essay over time. Write a rough draft during the summer before your senior year, and edit your work with the help of a teacher or your college guidance counselor. Remember that while you want someone else to read over the essay for mistakes and for a second opinion, you must write the essay. Here are some more tips:

- **Organize before writing.** (You know this strategy from your school assignments.) Don't just sit down to write—create an outline, write your ideas on note cards and order them, dictate your thoughts into a tape recorder. The more organized you are, the more smoothly the essay will go.

- **Capture admissions officers' attention** with a catchy opening and set your essay apart. (But avoid famous quotes, as they tend to be overused in college essays.)

- **Use descriptive images and details** to show your points rather than simply telling them to the reader.

- **Use vivid, related examples** that help the admissions office understand you and what you have to offer.

- **Write like yourself**—don't try to be someone you're not, and don't get so much help that the essay is clearly not your creation.

- **Proofread your essay** so there aren't any errors. (Watch out for spell-check—"candy striper" can easily become "candy stripper." Spell-check won't catch that. An admissions officer will.)

- **Ask others to read your essay.** English teachers, parents, and guidance counselors are excellent resources. They can check if your writing is compelling and descriptive and that your grammar is correct. They know you and can make sure that you sound like you in your essay.

HEADS UP ❗ Don't let someone else "write" your essay. Remember that the college is most likely going to see the scores you earned on the essay portion of the SAT or possibly on the optional writing section on the ACT. An essay that is wildly discrepant with your essay on the SAT or ACT is a warning bell for the admissions committees that the essay is not your own work.

CLEAN UP YOUR ONLINE PROFILE

Even before you start working on the essay, consider what your online profile is like. If you've posted pictures or comments on social networking sites that wouldn't sit well with an admissions committee, take the posts and photos down immediately. Some admissions officers (a small percentage) look at social networking websites when making decisions about applicants. A recent study of college admissions officers' searches of applicants' social networking profiles found that more often than not, these sites negatively rather than positively affected the admissions staff's view of the applicants. While admissions officers don't have time to check out the sites of each and every applicant, they may look at online profiles if they have doubts about an applicant. The best rule of thumb is to delete anything that doesn't speak well of you before you enter senior year. (This is a good rule of thumb outside of college admissions, too!)

SAMPLE ESSAY

On page 100 is an essay a student wrote for his college application. This student, who was admitted to a prestigious college, wrote about how he had overcome his challenges in high school to develop diligence and self-confidence. Notice that he didn't outright mention that he had a learning disability, but he did explain—using vivid, personal examples—how he had bettered himself and his work habits in high school.

SAMPLE ESSAY

The week before my history research paper was due in ninth grade, I dropped my box of index cards in front of my teacher's door. I had been carrying around the index cards for two weeks, but I was uncertain about how to take these unconnected bits of information, carefully paraphrased from my sources, and turn them into a coherent paper on the Bolsheviks. It was that drop of my cards that convinced me I had to change my tactics. The next day, I let my teacher know about my uncertainty, and we worked together to place the cards into an order that, along with connecting phrases, turned a series of white cards into a finished paper.

Since that time, I have realized that asking for help can be a strength. Now, I meet with my teachers in order to fully understand the material. At home each evening, I carefully go over my work and am very responsible with keeping up with the reading and getting assignments in on time. At school, I am willing to push myself and am taking more than the maximum amount of credits. I had to get permission from the head of the high school in order to maintain this course load. Even though I am eligible for a foreign language waiver, I refused to take the easy way out. Instead, I have taken French for six and a half years and have been able to excel in it. The Creative Writing class I took last semester has been a great source of pride for me. Writing has always been difficult for me, but in this class, I gained confidence in myself as a writer and actually began to enjoy the process. Just this spring, one of my creative writing stories won an award in a national writing competition.

I enjoy working hard and am proud that despite my learning issues, I have succeeded in high school. I have learned that a disappointment is not the end of the world but a chance to take a step back and evaluate what I need to work on. Something that took me a while to understand is that it's all right to ask for help. I have worked hard to have confidence in myself and to know that I have tried my best. I have found that if I believe I can do something and am prepared to work for it that I am quite capable of doing it. I now realize that dropping my index cards in front of my teacher's door in ninth grade was a fortunate accident that has helped me succeed.

COMPLETE APPLICATION SUPPLEMENTS

These types of additional material may be particularly important if you are the type of student who has a lot of talents, not all of which are in the classroom. Remember that extracurricular activities allow you to show colleges how you can add to their campus life. If you are very strong in an extracurricular area, you should strongly consider including supplements to your application. You should only submit these types of supplements if you have conscientiously dedicated yourself to an extracurricular activity (going to a few meetings of a club doesn't count). Also, keep in mind that colleges generally provide guidelines about which supplemental items they'll accept.

Supplemental Letter About Your ADD or LD

While you don't necessarily need to write your college essay about having ADD or learning disabilities, you can attach a supplementary letter to the college admissions office that goes along with your application. This letter can explain:

- what learning issues you've dealt with,
- how these issues may have affected your high school record,
- how you've overcome these issues, and
- how you plan to handle them in college.

FAMILY STRESS

Applying to college is a very stressful process for many people, and it is natural to feel a bit stressed out. After all, you're trying to plan for your life after high school, most likely the first time you will be independent from your parents. College costs a great deal of money, too, and you have to go through a difficult, time-consuming application process while still completing your senior year of high school. Many students find the college application process to be a source of tension with their parents, who may have very different ideas of what kinds of colleges their kids should attend. The time between submitting your applications and hearing back from schools can be particularly worrying for some students. If you are feeling stressed out, know that you are not alone. You may want to consult a trusted friend, counselor, or other important person in your life as you and your parents work your way through the process.

Keep in mind that you must show that you've worked to handle your issues and to develop a plan to navigate around them—and even to use them to your advantage—if you plan to write this type of letter. You may want to consult with a guidance counselor to help you think through the formulation of this type of letter. (See the earlier section under "SWOT Analysis" to determine whether or not you should reveal that you have ADD or LD to college admissions offices.)

Supplemental Materials to Submit

In addition to deciding whether to submit a letter explaining your ADD or LD, you should also consider submitting the following types of extra material:

- **If you're an athlete,** send a coach's letter and/or a DVD of yourself playing. (The Common Application has an athletic supplement.)

- **If you're an artist,** send slides or a CD or DVD of your work. (The Common Application has an arts supplement you can use.)

- **If you're a musician,** send a CD of yourself performing.

- **If you're involved in theater,** send a DVD of yourself performing, or a DVD or CD of your set designs or shows you've directed.

- **If you're a dancer,** send a DVD of a performance.

- **If you've done a lot of work on scientific research,** send in a sample of your research and analysis.

CHAPTER 12

TACKLE MONEY MATTERS

College is an expensive proposition. The tuition is only part of the cost of attending college. You and your family also have to consider your living expenses, including meals, trips home, clothes, entertainment, and books. You should sit down with your family and come up with a realistic budget—one that you can live with and that your parents can afford—before filling out the financial aid forms that are required as part of the college application process.

Financial Aid

Before applying for financial aid, you and your family should carefully weigh the amount of loans they want to take on and consider the other costs you will have as a student in college.

- **Know what your family can afford.**
- **Consider whether you will need to pay a lot for traveling** (plane, train, or car) back and forth to your school.
- **Add the cost of any additional services you may need** (tutoring not covered by the college, medication, doctors' visits, etc.) to the cost of your education.
- **Ask yourself whether the school you plan to attend is really worth the money.** Your family may have saved

money in what is called a 529 savings account for your college tuition, but these savings still don't cover the costs of college for many families.

HEADS UP ❗ How do you know you're getting the most for your tuition? Well, before you accept admission at a school, be sure that it will provide you with solid skills that are advantageous in the job market and for what you need in future years. Check what the school's job-placement record is for graduates, as well as what percentage of students graduate within four years.

FAFSA & PROFILE

Be sure to complete the Free Application for Federal Student Aid (FAFSA) as soon as possible, as a great deal of aid is given out on a first-come, first-served basis. It is available after January 1 of every year at www.fafsa.ed.gov. This form is used not only to determine federal aid but also to apply for state grants and college scholarships. Your college guidance counselor or financial aid officer can tell you how to apply and how to best complete this form.

Some colleges also require the CSS/Financial Aid PROFILE. PROFILE is an online application that collects information used by certain colleges and scholarship programs to award institutional funds (not federal funds like the FAFSA). You can file the PROFILE the fall before you'll be starting school (i.e., if you're starting school in fall 2011, you can apply as early as October 1, 2010). Keep in mind that every college has different deadlines, so make sure you check with each school and put the deadline on your calendar. You can apply on the College Board website.

Scholarships

In addition, there is some aid available to students with learning disabilities through a number of private scholarships. That's right—you are eligible for a number of private grants because you have LD or ADD. Be sure to consult the sources in the resources section of the book. Visit websites, such as the College Board's, to search databases of available scholarships, and be sure to speak to your college guidance counselor. You can also contact local community groups about scholarships that they may offer. Most scholarships require you to meet certain criteria, so be sure you meet their requirements and that you submit your requests for scholarships in advance of the deadlines. Organizations that grant scholarships usually have some additional requirements, other than submitting an application. Here are a few such requirements, just to give you an idea:

- **You may have to write essays** pertinent to the organization sponsoring the scholarship.

- **You might have to go on interviews** to be considered for certain scholarships.

In addition, beware of scams, such as scholarships that require fees for consideration. The Federal Trade Commission maintains a website of these scams.

CHAPTER 13

GO ON INTERVIEWS

To gain admission at many colleges, you will need to have an interview conducted by a graduate of that school or a member of the admissions staff. The interview is your chance to showcase your winning personality and give more dimension to your application. If you are nervous about the interview, the key to calming your jitters is practice and preparation.

HEADS UP ▉ The interview requires some practice. In fact, you may want to schedule practice interviews at schools you're not as interested in first—leaving the interviews at your dream schools for later in the admissions season when you are more practiced at the art of interviewing.

Interview Preparation

You will need to do some research before the interview. Remember those questions you developed for your college visits? Some of them would make great additions to your interview. By asking thoughtful questions, you show interest in the school.

In addition, you should research the school thoroughly so that you can let the interviewer know what specifically interests you in their school. The admissions staff wants to know that you will attend the school if admitted, so be sure to show particular interest in each school by doing some research and speaking knowledgeably in the interview.

- **You may not want to ask questions that reveal that you have ADD or LD,** but you want to ask thoughtful questions that show the interviewer that you want to be a conscientious student. For example, you can ask, "What kinds of tutoring do you provide at the tutoring center?" or "How do students at your school meet with professors if they want more information or have questions after class?"

- **You can ask about the college's resources to further your areas of interest**—whether you are interested in music, drama, economics, athletics, or other extracurricular areas. For example, you can ask, "I am very interested in your undergraduate business program, which I read is one of the best in the country. Can you tell me how students get into that program, and when that admission process takes place?"

- **Avoid vague questions** that can be easily found through online research, such as, "What's your music department like?"

- **Concentrate on more substantial queries,** such as, "What kinds of courses would be open to a first-year student who's interested in history?"

In preparing for an interview, you might get nervous. That's normal. Here are some ways to get ready for the actual one-on-one interview format:

- **Practice a mock interview with a friend or teacher.** You will learn ways to calm your nerves.

- **Practice speaking about yourself** in a way that isn't either boastful or self-deprecating.

- **Concentrate on not saying "um," "like," or "you**

TYPICAL INTERVIEW QUESTIONS:

- Describe an experience in high school that has significance for you.

- What is your family like?

- What activities do you participate in outside of classes?

- What kinds of books and magazines do you read?

know" when you talk. The less you do so in your everyday speech, the less likely you're to use these words in your interview.

- **Rehearse in front of a mirror** or make a movie of yourself to see how you really sound and look to interviewers.

Ready, Set, Interview!

There are a lot of things you can do to prepare for your interview. Here are some steps you can take to get ready for the big day:

1. Become familiar with the schools you are applying to through the research process you already went through above.

2. Conduct mock interviews with a trusted friend, teacher, or family member.

3. Write about how you will discuss your strengths and the challenges you've faced in school (remember your SWOT analysis?).

4. Write about your favorite book, academic subject, and the interests you want the interviewer to know about. Why do you like the books and subjects that you do?

5. How are you going to answer the question, "Why do you want to attend this college?" Consider specifics about professors, areas of study, or other features of this college that draw you to the school. Practice this answer for each college interview you attend, and be sure you are specific about that college. (Don't mention proximity to a city at a rural campus, for example.)

6. Work on your interview skills. What are some potential challenges you face? Do you fidget a lot? Do you have problems maintaining eye contact?

7. Select an appropriate outfit for your interview. No, you don't need to wear a suit, but dress professionally and neatly. This is not the time for jeans and a t-shirt.

If your interview doesn't go well at first, don't be disappointed. Step back, consider how you could do better and practice!

Get Interviewed

Interviews can be stressful for everyone. If you're not used to them or if you have trouble talking to others, the interview process can be even more intimidating. Students with non-verbal learning disorders or other similar disabilities may need particular practice preparing for the interview. But take heart. There are some straightforward strategies you can use to make your interview go more smoothly. Here are some tips:

- **Try to relax.** Don't forget to smile. You should have a good conversation with the interviewer. Admissions staff are, after all, used to speaking to college-bound students.

- **Take deep breaths** before the interview to calm yourself down if you get nervous. You can even ask a parent or sibling for a pep talk.

- **If you need time to answer a question,** just say, "Let me think about that." Interviewers don't mind waiting for you to consider your answer—it makes you look thoughtful!

- **Look the interviewer in the eye.**

- **It's all right for you to bring a list of questions** or reminders on a small index card with you to the interview if you think you will forget information.

- **Think about your responses ahead of time** without sounding too canned or rehearsed.

- **Most important, be yourself.** You will relax once you start speaking about subjects that interest you.

HEADS UP ! After your interview, be sure to write a short thank-you note to your interviewer (ask for his or her address during the interview). In your note, mention again what attracts you to the college, and thank the person for his or her time. You can even have a parent or teacher proofread your note. Be sure to use formal language and correct spelling and punctuation.

Here's one final note on interviewing. While many students find the interview process a little intimidating, remember it is just like going on a date with a talkative person. It is the job of interviewers to make you feel comfortable. So, all you have to do is dress up in clothes that make you feel and look good, take a deep breath, and speak about yourself and your interests in a poised way. After speaking about yourself for a few minutes, you may even find yourself enjoying the experience. After all, the subject (you!) is pretty interesting.

SENIOR YEAR: SPRING

MAKING DECISIONS

Around the end of March or beginning of April (unless you applied early decision or early action), you will start to hear back from the colleges you applied to. Unlike in the past, when students were either accepted or rejected, more and more students today are being placed on wait lists. That is, there are now three possible outcomes to the college application process: acceptance, rejection, and the wait list. You may find yourself faced with deciding on a school when you have some clear acceptances and still remain on the wait lists of other schools you'd like to attend. This section will help navigate these types of situations. No matter how your situation ends up, you should know that you have options and that you can find ways to pursue your education.

CHAPTER 14
DEAL WITH REJECTION

If you did not gain acceptance to your first-choice college, take heart. You are not alone. A lot of very successful people were rejected by Harvard—including investor Warren Buffett, anchorwoman Meredith Viera, CNN founder Ted Turner, and *The Simpsons* creator Matt Groening. That list shows you that admissions committees can't take every excellent applicant—they just can't. In addition, they are using only limited information to make their choices. Most people don't reach their potential by age 18, and remember that the best years lie ahead for you. You will bring the qualities that set you apart to whatever college you choose to attend. Remember that study that showed people who were admitted to Ivy League colleges but chose not to attend were just as successful as those who had attended these schools? This study shows that people bring their qualities with them wherever they go. College doesn't make you—instead, you make your college years count.

If you haven't gained admission to a college you want to attend, you have a lot of options.

- **Consider taking a gap year** to build on your academic skills or your life experiences. You will head to college more mature and better able to handle the challenges of school. In fact, students who take a gap year tend to do better in college.

- Consider attending a two-year college—perhaps close to home—to bolster your skills before transferring to a four-year school. An associate's degree will give you two more years to build your academic portfolio. A lot of very successful people have attended junior colleges and then gone on to graduate from a four-year college.

- **Look at trade schools.** These types of institutions, often called vocational schools, can teach you marketable skills to prepare you for a career in nursing, culinary work, automotive work, paralegal work, technology, fashion, and other fields. Be sure that the school you choose places its graduates in paid jobs.

- **Get a job.** You can find a good job without going to college. Many licensed trades, such as electricians and plumbers, require apprenticeships rather than a college degree. You can often get on-the-job training without attending college, and these types of trades tend to pay well. You can also work at other types of jobs for a few years and attend college part-time or full-time after gaining some years of work and life experience.

Do not be discouraged. The fact that you have this book shows that you are driven and will get to college!

CHAPTER 15

TACKLE THE WAIT LIST

More and more colleges are wait-listing a great deal of their applicants because the schools are unsure about which of their accepted students will actually attend the school. Once admitted students respond to a college, the school starts taking students off their wait list to fill out their remaining spaces. In recent years, a large number of students have been accepted from the wait lists of colleges (even prestigious colleges). The wait list process can drag out through the summer before your first year of college.

This section will help you evaluate whether you should pursue being admitted to a college if you are on the wait list. Here are some things to know about the wait list:

- **You can't be sure of getting in off the wait list,** so, if possible, you need to make sure you have a college to attend.

- **You have to reply to a school that has accepted you** usually by May 1 (check the exact deadline). Send in a deposit to secure a place at a college.

- **Being wait-listed is not the same as being rejected.** In fact, recent statistics from the National Association for College Admission Counseling (NACAC) show that almost a third of students who are wait listed wind up gaining admissions to that college.

- **You can choose to remain on the wait list or remove yourself from the wait list.** Be sure to let colleges you want to attend know that you are interested in remaining on the wait list, and contact them as soon as possible.

- **You can elect to stay on more than one wait list.**

Here are some strategies you can use to increase your chances of being admitted off the wait list:

- **Don't constantly e-mail or call the college that wait-listed you.** College admissions officers do not enjoy being pestered. They will ignore any flowers, chocolate, or gag gifts you send them.

- **If you have a new achievement colleges should know about** (such as an award you earned at the end of your senior year or at graduation), be sure to let them know by writing them a letter.

- **Request an interview,** if you didn't have one when you were initially applying. Personal contact with the admissions office might give them a better idea of who you are and what you would bring to their school.

- **You can have a person who is connected to the college contact the admissions staff.** For example, if you know an alumnus of the school, have this person write to the admissions staff about what a great fit you are with the college and how much you want to attend.

- **Some colleges will give you a sense of whether you are at the top or the bottom** of the wait list. If you are at the very bottom, it's probably not worth your while to remain on the wait list. However, if you are near the top, you have a good shot at admission.

- **If you are only wait-listed but have no definite acceptances,** be sure to line up what you are going to do next year in case you aren't taken off any wait lists. For example, arrange to take a gap year or enroll at a community college to ensure you have somewhere to go in the fall.

- **If you are admitted off the wait list at one college but not at the college you really want to attend,** call your top-choice school to let them know. They may tell you that you are close to admission, and the information that you've been accepted to another school can help them decide (hopefully in your favor) more quickly.

- **Figure out, before deciding to accept admission, if your late acceptance affects your housing or anything else about your admission.** For example, if you are admitted from the wait list, will you still be eligible for financial aid and for preference in housing? Ask these questions before deciding to accept admission.

If you've been wait-listed at one or a few schools, it can be stressful. After all, you're waiting! A plan can help make this process more manageable. On the next page is a timeline to help you navigate the wait-list process and figure out where to go from there. You'll notice that no specific months are given, except for the first one—May. That's because you can remain on wait lists through the summer before your first year of college, and you can be taken off the wait list as early as May.

WAIT LIST TIMELINE

By May 1	• Accept admission and send in a deposit to a college that has admitted you
As soon as you hear you've been wait-listed	• Contact schools to let them know you want to remain on the wait list • Remove yourself from wait lists that you don't want to remain on • Request interviews at schools that wait-listed you and at which you did not interview before • Send schools at which you are wait-listed supplemental material about achievements they do not know about
When admitted off the wait list	• Investigate whether you will receive financial aid • Let the school you accepted admission to in May know about your decision

CHAPTER 16

CHOOSE YOUR SCHOOL

If you've been admitted to a few schools, now's the time to choose which one you really want to attend. You have to send in a deposit and an acceptance to a school generally by May 1, even if you are on the wait list at other schools. Be sure to send in your deposit to a school to be sure you have a place. How do you decide on the school you want to attend? Here are some guidelines:

- **Look clearly at the criteria you selected when you were researching schools** (remember fall of junior year?). Although your criteria may have changed as you researched colleges (and changing your mind is part of the process), remind yourself what's really important to you and what are your top (mature) priorities.

- **If you don't know whether your admission choices meet your needs,** go back and get answers from the college. It's normal and acceptable for you to do your research in waves.

- **If you haven't found out answers about what your college choices offer**—whether it's work study opportunities, a tutoring center, or other needs—the time to ask is now, before you choose where you want to go.

- **If you need financial aid** (or even if you don't), compare the total cost of attending each college.

HEADS UP ! Don't ignore that gut feeling you have about which college is right for you. There is a role that instinct and emotion play in choosing a college. You should without a doubt factor in the way you felt at the colleges you visited and the way you think you would feel attending each college. Go back to your notes and pictures you took at each college. Remember, you also need to sort out well-informed perceptions of a college from snap judgments based on superficialities, such as a college's mascot, ranking in national polls, football team, or reputation as a party school.

Determine if Colleges Meet Your Needs

Use the chart below to see how your choices measure up to your top five priorities. In the left-hand column,

PRIORITY CHECK CHART

TOP PRIORITY	COLLEGE #1	COLLEGE #2
1. Urban campus	no—middle of nowhere!	yes—in L.A.!
2. Strong music program	yes—renowned for it	kind of—but not as strong as I'd like
3. Financial aid	good package	too much debt
4. Strong writing and tutoring center	writing center, but students pay for tutoring	writing center, but always crowded
5. Study abroad program	no, but offers credit for other colleges' programs	great study abroad program in Italy

write your top priorities from the list you composed. Then, check whether each college meets those priorities. You can either use check marks or Xs or "yes" or "no," or you can grade each potential college on how well they meet your criteria. You can use this chart as a template to create your own.

I Made My Decision. Now What?

So you've picked your college. Congratulations! Here is what you need to do to finish up the application process.

- **Accept admission to your college of choice.** This is done by submitting a deposit, usually by May 1 (check the deadlines).

- **Send letters declining admission to all the other**

COLLEGE #3	COLLEGE #4	COLLEGE #5
no—on a farm	sort of—in the suburbs	yes—in Chicago
no—more of a drama program	yes—affiliation with local symphony	nope
good package, but requires work study	little aid, but lower tuition	full ride!
help from professors, but no writing or tutoring center	help from TAs	writing and tutoring center
no—hard to get credit for study abroad	study abroad programs in many countries	study abroad but not for credit

schools you got into. (You can find samples of these letters online.)

- If you were wait-listed anywhere, send letters withdrawing yourself from the wait list if you do not want to attend those schools.

- If you applied early admission, send letters withdrawing your application to the other colleges to which you had applied regular admission.

If you are satisfied with your choice, congratulations! You are now on your way to school, and you can comfortably buy your college sweatshirt.

CONCLUSION

Congratulations! You've now made it through the difficult admission process. By figuring out how you can leverage your strengths, you are well on way to becoming a successful college student. That's right—you've already done a great deal of the work that will be required of you in college. While you will still have to study for exams and write papers, you've sorted through a whole lot of information to find out what's most important to you. Just as important, you know how to capitalize on your strengths, overcome or work with your weaknesses, and plan for your future.

Take a look at the appendix to get a glimpse at what you can do this summer before you head off to school. You'll get a leg up on your first semester!

Now you are ready to really engage with a college program that you will find fun and rewarding. Enjoy your journey and good luck!

SUMMER BEFORE COLLEGE

This section covers steps you should take before you reach your college campus to make sure that you hit the ground running in the fall. To make sure your first semester goes well, you should use the lazy days of summer to get your documentation together to ask for accommodations, line up any medication you need, and set up some guidelines with your parents for your new independent college life.

REQUEST ACCOMMODATIONS

Students should approach the office of students with disabilities (this office has different names at different colleges) right after accepting admission—the sooner the better. Before admission, you conducted research about which accommodations the colleges offer, and before your first semester is in session, contact the office of students with disabilities. Sorting out your accommodations before you start classes in the fall of your first year will let you start school without the additional burden of working out your accommodations.

If you plan to visit your school during pre-freshman week or during the summer after you graduate, before you arrive on campus, sort out your accommodations then. It's the perfect time to get your accommodations all lined up. Contact the office that handles requests well in

ACCOMMODATION REQUEST CHECKLIST

- ☐ Contact office of students with disabilities
- ☐ Research requirements for accommodations
- ☐ Provide documentation of long-standing disability
- ☐ Provide documentation of major effects of disability

advance of your visit (at least one week and preferably more), and ask if you can meet with someone in the office who can help you.

There are a lot of components to requesting accommodations, so it's best to be very organized.

Submit Documentation

Each college has different requirements. Be sure to check the documentation requirements on the college's website. Generally, they want to see two things:

- Proof of a long-standing disability

- Evidence that the disability has had and continues to have a major effect on your life and your ability to learn

Keep in mind that colleges don't follow the same rules that high schools do for granting accommodations. While colleges and high schools grant accommodations under the Americans with Disabilities Act (ADA) of 1990 and Section 504 of the 1973 Rehabilitation Act, colleges can offer "reasonable accommodations" and don't have to change their curricula to meet the needs of students with learning disabilities. In addition, these rules may or may not apply to colleges run by religious organizations, so be sure to check whether these rules apply if you are attending a school run by a religious institution.

LONG-STANDING DISABILITY

Colleges want to see that you've had a long-standing disability that has been re-evaluated within the last three years. Generally, ADD and learning disabilities have to be documented in an educational evaluation conducted by a licensed psychologist or neuropsychologist or similar professional. Here are a few rules of thumb:

- **Colleges are more likely to provide accommodations** if you've documented that you had a disability starting in the earlier grades.

- **They are more reluctant in general to grant accommodations** to people who've first been evaluated towards the end of their high school careers. This policy arises because the colleges are wary of granting accommodations to people who are trying to game the system and only get accommodations for standardized testing. Make sure your evaluation records the long-standing nature and lengthy documented history of your ADD or LD.

The documentation for proving a long-term disability varies from college to college, but here is what you'll most likely need:

- intelligence tests

- achievement tests that demonstrate a gap between ability and achievement due to LD or ADD

- a background and academic history of the student

- evidence that the learning issues or ADD affect the student's learning

- other tests may be required

EFFECTS OF THE DISABILITY

Colleges want to see evidence that your ADD or LD affects major life activities or imposes functional limitations on you. So, if you have a disability but continue to perform very well on academic and other tasks, the college may be more reluctant to grant you accommodations.

You may need outside documentation, such as testing from a psychologist or neuropsychologist, and not just from your school.

Visit the Jutoring Center

Before you start school, you may also want to visit the tutoring center, or at least look on your college's website to find out the help they offer. Some departments have professors, graduate students, or fellow students who offer tutoring, and the library may also offer study groups. Find out how you sign up for appointments for tutoring and how far in advance you need to do so.

MORE SUMMER PLANNING

In addition to arranging for your accommodations, you should set up your medical care at college. You should also tackle the sometimes difficult—though always necessary—conversation with your parents about how you will keep in touch with them once you start college.

Get Your Meds in Line

Are you on medication for your ADD (or for other issues)? If you have medical needs, here are some things to consider the summer before school starts and you get really busy. The earlier you do this sort of planning, the better.

- **Figure out if your hometown doctor can serve your needs during your time at college.**

- **If you are going to be far from home,** you might need to set up an appointment with a nurse or doctor at your school's health center.

- **Consider how you are going to get the medication you need away from home,** and whether you can fill prescriptions at your college.

- **You also may want to arrange to meet with a doctor or mental health counselor** at school if you will need regular appointments with these professionals during the school year.

- **Determine what health insurance plan you will use.** Many students can stay on their parents' health insurance plans until they are 25. If you are over 25,

or you can't use your parents' health insurance (or
they don't have coverage), check out the health insurance plans offered by the college or university you will
be attending. Some students may also be eligible for
Medicaid or state-sponsored insurance pools.

ABUSING STIMULANT MEDICATION

Simply put: don't. Taking any kind of medication
always carries risks. Stimulants can be addictive
for those who aren't prescribed the medication.
There are also side effects, including insomnia,
heart palpitations, and even cardiovascular problems. If you (or your parents) are concerned about
abuse of stimulant medication, ask your doctor
about some of the newer non-stimulant ADD medi-
cations that can't be abused.

Deal With Your Parents

Soon you might not be living at home any more, but
your parents will still be your parents. And you will still
be their child. The summer before you head off to college
is the time to figure out how to deal with life's ups and
downs on your own. Ask your parents to allow you to do
so, too. College is an introduction to the independence of
adulthood. It's the perfect time to try to work out your
life on your own (with some help from trusted friends,
professors, or deans). So, you need to plan how you will
maintain your relationship with them and still be an independent college student.

Here are some tips:

- **Negotiate ahead of time how you will communicate** with your parents if you are attending school away from home. Choose times and frequencies for calls that are convenient for everyone.

- **Adjust how you share news with your parents now—** and try not to depend on them so much when something goes wrong. That way, when you get to school, you won't give in to the impulse to call your parents every time you lose your keys or get into an argument with your roommates (or even if you get an A on a paper or make the swim team).

- **Speak with your parents about what your budget is** and which kinds of purchases, such as textbooks and class materials, are your responsibility.

Some advance work on lining up your accommodations and medical care over the summer before college starts means that you can start school with confidence. You've done the legwork necessary to ensure that you have everything in place for a great first semester.

ADDITIONAL RESOuRCES

For Researching Colleges

BOOKS

The lists in these books are not a complete list of all the schools that can accommodate students with learning disabilities and at which such students can be successful. You can attend a college that isn't on these lists if you think it's a good match for you.

Colleges for Students with Learning Disabilities or AD/HD, 8th Edition. (2007). Lawrenceville, NJ: Peterson's.

Pope, Loren. (2006). *Colleges That Change Lives: 40 Schools That Will Change the Way You Think About Colleges.* New York, NY: Penguin.

Princeton Review, Marybeth Kravets, & Imy Wax. (2010). *The K&W Guide to Colleges for Students with Learning Disabilities, 10th edition.* New York, NY: Princeton Review

This guide provides extensive information about some colleges with services for students with learning disabilities.

For Applying to Colleges

BOOKS

Springer, Sally P., Jon Reider, & Marion R. Franck. (2009). *Admission Matters: What Students and Parents Need to Know About Getting into College.* New York, NY: Jossey-Bass.

WEBSITES

The College Board
www.collegeboard.com

The College Board is the organization that administers the SAT I and Subject Tests and the Advanced Placement (AP) tests. Their website provides information about how to ask for accommodations on their tests, including their requirements for documentation.

ACT
www.actstudent.org

This is the website for the administration that administers the ACT. Their website contains information about how to request accommodations on the ACT, including their requirements for documentation.

The National Center for Fair & Open Testing
www.fairtest.org

This website has a list of colleges/universities that do not require the SAT or ACT for admission.

The Common Application
www.commonapp.org

At this website, you can download the forms for the Common Application and find out which colleges and universities accept the Common Application.

For Scholarship & Financial Information

BOOKS

Kaplan, Ben. (2001). *How to Go to College Almost For Free*. New York, NY: Collins Reference.

The College Board. *Scholarship Handbook*.Princeton, NJ: College Board.

Published by the College Board and updated annually, this book includes scholarships for students with disabilities.

WEBSITES

Free Application for Federal Student Aid www.fafsa.ed.gov

Access the Free Application for Federal Student Aid (FAFSA).

City of College Dreams www.cityofcollegedreams.org

A great resource about how to reduce the cost of tuition and afford the school of your dreams.

For Transitioning to College

BOOKS

Quinn, Patricia O. (ed.) (2001). *ADD and the College Student: A Guide for High School and College Students with Attention Deficit Disorder*. Washington, DC: Magination Press.

Nadeau, Kathleen. (2006). *Survival Guide for College Students With ADHD or LD, Second Edition*. Washington, DC: Magination Press.

Mooney, Jonathan, & David Cole. (2000). *Learning Outside the Lines: Two Ivy League Students with Learning Disabilities and ADHD Give You the Tools for Academic Success and Educational Revolution*. New York, NY: Simon and Schuster.

For Considering a Gap Year

BOOKS

White, Kristin M. (2009). *The Complete Guide to the Gap Year: The Best Things to Do Between High School and College.* New York, NY: Jossey-Bass.

WEBSITES

Gapyear.com
www.gapyear.com

This site provides you with ideas for a gap year and helps you plan for your trip. In addition, there are message boards to connect with fellow students who are on a gap year.

Planet Gap Year
www.planetgapyear.com

This site allows you to search a database with options for your gap year, and it features writing by students who are traveling during their gap year.

Additional Info

National Collegiate Athletic Association
www.ncaa.org

You can find the eligibility requirements for college-bound student-athletes.

ABOUT THE AUTHOR

Blythe Grossberg, PsyD, is a learning specialist in New York City who works to help children and adults with ADD become more effective at school and at work. She has worked for over a decade with middle and high school students with learning issues, such as ADD, language and reading disorders, spatial and math disorders, Asperger's syndrome, and others, to help them get organized, succeed in school, and perform on standardized tests. Dr. Grossberg is the author of *Making ADD Work: On-the-Job Strategies for Coping with Attention Deficit Disorder* and *Test Success: Test-Taking and Study Strategies for All Students, Including those with ADD and LD*. A graduate of Harvard College and Rutgers Graduate School of Applied and Professional Psychology, she has written for *Boston Magazine, ADDitude Magazine, New York Times* supplements, and other publications. She has spoken before the Manhattan Adult ADD Support Group and CHADD (Children and Adults with ADD). Her work has also been featured on ADDManagement.com and other websites for people with ADD.

ABOUT MAGINATION PRESS

Magination Press publishes self-help books for kids and the adults in their lives. We are an imprint of the American Psychological Association, the largest scientific and professional organization representing psychologists in the United States and the largest association of psychologists worldwide.